D1685761

PENNY FRANCIS

FOREWORD BY BISHOP JOHN FRANCIS

My
affliction
has a

SOUND

Discover the powerful connection
between sound and our suffering

Other Titles
By The Author

Your First Steps

From Pen to Paper

Shame Is Not Your Portion

For more information visit:

www.pastorpennyfrancis.com

Print ISBN: 978-0-9957999-4-3
www.pastorpennyfrancis.com

All Scripture quotations, unless otherwise indicated are taken
from the Holy Bible, King James Version.

Graphics by Justin Foster

Dedication

This book is dedicated to my husband, Bishop John Francis— my biggest fan! I decided to dedicate this book to him because he asked me to write it! He kept talking about a message I preached at our church and every time he kept saying, you should write the book — So I did!

We have been married for nearly 30 years and he has always celebrated me and has wished, prayed and hoped that this literary piece would happen. He has watched me write so many pieces on so many occasions but never for myself. This time he is so excited that I have finally taken the time to make this happen.

John, you saw so much more in me than I saw in myself. Thank you for never giving up on me — for your persistence and insistence but most of all thank you for trusting my gift. You know I have a passion for writing but just knowing that this book was one that you particularly wanted me to write helped me to keep typing. You never stopped talking about me writing this book and it worked — Darling, I wrote the book! I hope you enjoy reading it.

Thank you for pushing me firmly but gently so my dreams could come true too. I love you, forever and always.

I also dedicate this book to my daughters, Juanita, Teleisa and Charisa — my three angels. Thank you so much for your encouraging words. I love and appreciate all three of you. Never lose your uniqueness and individuality — it's your strength. I hope when you hold this book in your hands and read it, that you will remember to never give up on your dreams no matter how long they take to materialise. My love always,

To my sister, Paula, my brother, Philip and my niece and nephew, Panache and Pierson. Thanks for understanding the pull of ministry on me and for all your unconditional love... Love you loads.

To the family who I don't see as often... We may be separated by distance and circumstances but every family life experience no matter how brief or small, has touched my life in some significant way.

To my mother, the late Ida Aurora Turner, who started me off writing. She would dictate her letters or should I say long epistles to me and I would have to make sure it had the right grammar and punctuation! 'Penny, go and get your pen and paper' she would say! And if I complained she would say, 'Why do you think I send you to school!' I can remember sitting at the table as a child on many occasions with the dictionary trying to find the right words to fit into the sentence I was constructing — Thanks Mum, for igniting my passion for writing. I know you would have loved to see this moment.

To my Dad, the late Herman James, how wonderful it was to have you back in my life and how sad I feel that you couldn't stay longer – 10 years wasn't enough. I know you would have been so proud of your Pen! Well, Dad, I finally put pen to paper! See you later Dad...

To Ruach City Church and friends thank you for your prayers, expressions of encouragement and continued interest. As promised, my first book – I hope you enjoy reading it! I know you were expecting the poetry one... Watch this space – it's on its way!

I couldn't finish this dedication without writing a few words in appreciation of my mother-in-law, the late Mother Elfreda Francis. A true mother in Zion but I just call her Mum! She was an encouragement to me in more ways than she knew. She was my shadow, routing for me in every service and smiling with pride as I ministered the Word. I will miss her affectionate slaps and her private parables of correction and wisdom. I miss not seeing her in my rear-view mirror as I drive to church. Thank you Mum for all your prayers and words of affirmation. God bless you always. Love you!

Foreword
By Bishop John Francis

I have been waiting to see this day — my wife has finally published this book. I've observed her over the years and I have seen her blossom and grow into this amazing woman. To be honest, I thought she was really amazing when I first met her over 30 years ago! In fact one of my first remarks was, 'he who finds you will obtain favour from God,' not knowing that I would be the one to have the privilege of this treasure in my life. I knew when I married her that she was a precious gem.

Apart from all the wonderful gifts and talents my wife has and there are many, she is an incredible communicator. I know this book will be life-changing for anyone who reads it, not just because Penny wrote it but because it's filled with revelation for life.

I am so glad to finally see her book in print and I'm really excited because I know there are more to come. I can't wait to see what else she's going to come out with. If you could see me right now, I have a big grin on my face! I could go on and on and on but I won't... Start reading — You won't be disappointed!

Penny Francis

My Affliction
Has A Sound

**Discover the powerful connection
between sound and our suffering**

Contents

Dedication
Foreword

Introduction

This book is birthed out of a couple of messages I preached at my church. The book actually carries the title of the message which was preached at our first Super Sunday Miracle & Healing Service in 2015. It was a powerful service and God moved amazingly and people were deeply touched and moved by the Word. After the service, my husband, Bishop John Francis said that I should write a book and when I thought about it, it seemed like a good idea. It has taken me a bit of a while to get round to writing it.

In 2016 I preached another message entitled 'There's a Purpose to My Affliction'. This book is a culmination of these two powerful messages. As you read, I do take you on quite a journey of research and discovery, which some of you may find questionable but hopefully you will enjoy these areas of exploration! When it comes to my study and research of the Bible I have never been a conformist. I like to see where my questions take me which the majority of the time can be quite interesting and fruitful. In essence 'My Affliction Has A Sound' is all about the powerful connection of sound to our seasons of difficulty and how God responds to the sounds of His people but we do embark on quite a scholarly and investigative voyage to get there.

I hope you enjoy observing from my perspective and come to a similar conclusion — simply that when we go through times of affliction, even when we don't cry or make an audible sound, we still cry... because our Affliction Has A Sound!

An Affliction Story

And the angel of the Lord said unto her, Behold, thou art with child, and shalt bear a son, and shalt call his name Ishmael; because the Lord hath heard thy affliction —Genesis 16:11

The backdrop and setting for this book is found in a Biblical story about a young woman's experience of affliction in Genesis 16 and refers to a series of events surrounding a woman called Hagar. She was a maid who belonged to Sarah, Abraham's wife. In her efforts to help God out with the promised arrival of her longed for baby, she suggested that Abraham sleep with her maid so that she would conceive. Her plan worked! Hagar conceives and becomes pregnant and begins to view her mistress differently. In fact the Bible states that she began to view Sarah with contempt (Genesis 16:5).

Jewish teachings (opinions of classical commentators and early rabbinic traditions) and also ancient near Eastern parallels help us gain some insight into the historical—social setting of the Torah. In general, these sources suggest that Hagar, now pregnant with Abraham's child, would have expected to become Abraham's main wife, replacing Sarah in seniority and privileges. Also, because Sarah was barren, it would have been assumed that Sarah was wicked and rejected by God.[1] When Sarah realises that the pregnancy has caused Hagar to despise her, she treats her very harshly so Hagar runs away (Genesis 16:6).

Some Biblical translations state that Sarah beat Hagar. Other commentaries provide additional insight stating that Sarah would have been very frustrated and would have struggled with this turn of events seeing Hagar pregnant while she was still barren, with no child. So she tormented Hagar and worked her harder than really necessary. Perhaps she also struck and cursed her until she could no longer tolerate it and in desperation fled.[2] This situation would have been further adversely impacted and caused some friction because the text states that Hagar was Egyptian and therefore not considered God's chosen.

> It would have been assumed that Sarah was wicked and rejected by God

So Hagar finds herself in the desert where the angel of the Lord speaks to her and tells her to return to her mistress and be obedient. She is also told that her descendants will be innumerable. That she is expecting a son and that she should name him Ishmael (Genesis 16:9-11). Imagine doing exactly what you have been told to do and then being severely punished for it.

The punishment meted out by Sarah must have been so severe as to cause her to leave the safety of her home and run away into the desert, especially as she was pregnant. She was vulnerable, wandering in the desert most probably trying to work out what she was going to do next. Her predicament is now precarious and she has nowhere to go. When the angel of the Lord speaks to Hagar in the desert she is at a very low point. He asks her what she is doing and she tells the angel that she is running away from Sarah (Genesis 16:8).

I can picture Hagar's face when she is told to return to Sarah and submit to her authority! After all that she had been through, I'm sure these were not the words she wanted to hear but she was obedient and returned to Sarah. Before Hagar leaves the desert the angel of the Lord tells her one more thing. He tells Hagar that the Lord has heard her affliction. As I read those words on that Super Sunday in 2015, they resonated in my spirit and my exploration into affliction began. I discovered that Hagar's story of affliction isn't the only one to be found in the Bible.

What Is Affliction?

The Nelson Bible Dictionary refers to affliction in simple terms as 'any condition or problem that produces suffering or pain'. The Hebrew translation for the word 'affliction', in this verse is `oniy' (pronounced on-ee')[3] which means depression, misery and trouble. It translates from another Hebrew word which gives us more insight into what affliction is — the idea of looking down or browbeating; to depress literally or figuratively, to weaken, in any wise.

Affliction in the Old Testament is seen as both individual (sickness, poverty, oppression by the strong and rich, perverted justice) and national. Study shows that great emphasis is given to affliction as a national experience in the Old Testament, due to calamities such as war, invasion, conquest by foreign peoples, exile, etc. In the New Testament the chief form of affliction is that due to the fierce antagonism manifested to the religion of Jesus, resulting in persecution of His followers and those who firmly adhered to His teachings.

One common question that the afflicted poses when suffering is 'why'? It's hard to compute that our benevolent and loving God would allow us to suffer in this way. One answer to this question is found in **Isaiah 48:10 — Behold, I have refined thee, but not with silver; I have chosen thee in the furnace of affliction.** The New Century Version provides us with more clarity, "I have made you pure, but not by fire, as silver is made pure. I have purified you by giving you troubles." It would seem that God defines one of the purposes to affliction as purification or a way of testing us.

Alternatively, according to an article on affliction in the International Standard Bible Encyclopedia, a common view in early Hebrew theology was that afflictions were the

It speaks...
It shouts...
It testifies...
It announces...
It sings...

result of the divine law of retribution, by which sin was invariably followed by adequate punishment. So then the people of the day saw every misfortune as a proof of the sufferer's sinfulness. This coincides with the attitude of Job's "friends", Eliphaz, Bildad and Zophar, towards him as they sought to convince him that his great sufferings were due to his sinfulness (Job 2:11-13; Job 4:7-8; Job 22:4-5). This is generally the standpoint of the historians of Israel, who regarded personal and national calamities as a mark of divine displeasure on account of the people's sins. However, when you look more closely, this generalist viewpoint is inadequate to cover all cases, e.g., Jeremiah's sufferings were not due to sin, but to his faithfulness to his prophetic vocation (Jeremiah 20:1-2; Jeremiah 26:11; Jeremiah 38:6). And despite all that Job suffered he stayed firm in the conviction of his own integrity. In fact he was quite adamant as is clear from his words in Job 27:

"I vow by the living God, who has taken away my rights, by the Almighty who has embittered my soul. As long as I live, while I have breath from God, my lips will speak no evil, and my tongue will speak no lies. I will never concede that you are right; I will defend my integrity until I die. I will maintain my innocence without wavering. My conscience is clear for as long as I live —Job 27:1-6 (New Living Translation)

I also learnt that affliction means 'to begin to speak; specifically to sing (together by course), shout, to say, to testify, to announce, to utter, to cause to give answer, to cry (Strong's Exhaustive Concordance #6030).

After reading about the meaning of affliction I came to the conclusion that affliction has a voice; our condition or state of difficulty has a voice. It speaks... It shouts... It testifies... It announces... It sings... For me, the logical next step in my thought process was to surmise that if my condition has a voice and speaks then shouldn't my affliction expect or require an answer or a response?

As I looked at the text, it seemed to me that this was what happened in the situation of Hagar because the Angel of the Lord told Hagar that He was sharing this information with her *because* the Lord had heard her affliction.

25

And the angel of the Lord said unto her, Behold, thou art with child, and shalt bear a son, and shalt call his name Ishmael; *because the Lord hath heard thy affliction*
—Genesis 16:11

So when Hagar was in that wilderness, in that desert place, I believe her affliction called out to God and the Lord responded. Hagar's story can be a source of encouragement and hope to us as believers to know that whenever we can't find the words to say or even when we feel we are stumbling clumsily through our prayers to God or it feels like our prayers are just bouncing off the ceiling — He hears and He responds. We can be crying and blubbering through our tears about how difficult or challenging a season is but I believe our affliction is speaking loudly and clearly and definitely in a language that God understands.

Affliction That Touches God's Heart

There are several references to the affliction experiences suffered by God's people that have been recorded in the Bible. Anyone who feels they are suffering or experiencing affliction can identify with these characters from the Bible. Job makes mention of how debilitating his season of suffering was — **My heart is troubled and restless. Waves of affliction have come upon me. I am black but not from sunburn. I stand up and cry to the assembly for help. (But I might as well save my breath), for I am considered a brother to jackals and a companion to ostriches. My skin is black and peeling. My bones burn with fever. The voice of joy and gladness has turned to mourning —Job 30:27-31 (The Living Bible).**

The accounts of experiences of the afflicted, pleas for help and moments of despair will touch our emotions in the deepest places. The following verses exhibit this: **Look upon mine affliction and my pain; and forgive all my sins — Psalm 25:18**

Consider mine affliction, and deliver me: for I do not forget thy law. Plead my cause, and deliver me: quicken me according to thy word —Psalm 119:153-154

The Scriptures abound in words of consolation and exhortation adapted to encourage the afflicted.

A popular consideration comes to mind — **All things work together for good to them that love God" —Romans 8:28.** It is also a comforting thought to know that our suffering is of brief duration, in comparison with the joy that shall follow — **For his anger endureth but a moment; in his favour is life: weeping may endure for a night, but joy cometh in the morning —Psalm 30:5.** The afflicted one is encouraged to rely on the mercies and kindness of their God — **For a small moment have I forsaken thee; but with great mercies will I gather thee. In a little wrath I hid my face from thee for a moment; but with everlasting kindness will I have mercy on thee, saith the Lord thy Redeemer —Isaiah 54:7-8.**

In spite of the plight of the afflicted we see, in the Bible, that the Lord will deliver His people — **And the patriarchs, moved with envy, sold Joseph into Egypt: but God was with him, and delivered him out of all his afflictions, and gave him favour and wisdom in the sight of Pharaoh king of Egypt; and he made him governor over Egypt and all his house —Acts 7:9-10.**

We also can learn from the experiences of the afflicted who are encouraged to fortify themselves in affliction remembering that **"the affliction is light and momentary compared with the "far more exceeding and eternal weight of glory" which is to issue out of the experience —2 Corinthians 4:17.** This is witnessed by the words of

28

Romans 8:18 — For I reckon that the sufferings of this present time are not worthy to be compared with the glory which shall be revealed in us. In the New Testament the Apostle Paul speaks about his afflictions but refuses to allow them to interfere with his apostolic assignment — **And now, behold, I go bound in the spirit unto Jerusalem, not knowing the things that shall befall me there: Save that the Holy Ghost witnesseth in every city, saying that bonds and afflictions abide me. But none of these things move me, neither count I my life dear unto myself, so that I might finish my course with joy, and the ministry, which I have received of the Lord Jesus, to testify the gospel of the grace of God —Acts 20:22-24.**

As followers of Christ we are instructed to conduct ourselves as integral ministers of God despite the suffering that we go through — **Giving no offence in any thing, that the ministry be not**

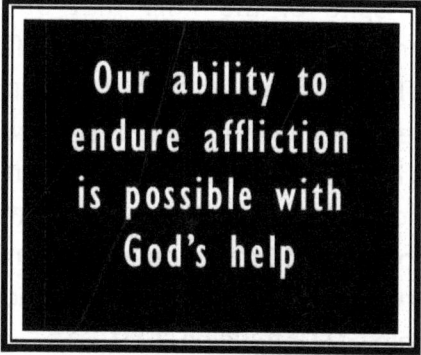

Our ability to endure affliction is possible with God's help

blamed: But in all things approving ourselves as the ministers of God, in much patience, in afflictions, in necessities, in distresses, In stripes, in imprisonments, in tumults, in labours, in watchings, in fastings; by pureness, by knowledge, by longsuffering, by kindness, by the Holy Ghost, by love unfeigned, by the word of truth, by the power of God, by the armour of righteousness on the right hand and on the left, by honour and dishonour, by

evil report and good report: as deceivers, and yet true; As unknown, and yet well known; as dying, and, behold, we live; as chastened, and not killed; As sorrowful, yet alway rejoicing; as poor, yet making many rich; as having nothing, and yet possessing all things —2 Corinthians 6:3-10.

It is interesting to note that our ability to endure affliction is possible with God's help; His divine power operating in us — **Be not thou therefore ashamed of the testimony of our Lord, nor of me his prisoner: but be thou partaker of the afflictions of the gospel according to the power of God —2 Timothy 1:8.**

In spite of the help that our God provides whilst an individual is going through affliction, the prayers of the afflicted often indicate their expectation that yes, God will hear and help but also that He will deliver them out of their affliction: **If, when evil cometh upon us, as the sword, judgment, or pestilence, or famine, we stand before this house, and in thy presence, (for thy name is in this house,) and cry unto thee in our affliction, then thou wilt hear and help —2 Chronicles 20:9**

Consider mine affliction, and deliver me: for I do not forget thy law —Psalm 119:153

I am afflicted very much: quicken me, O Lord, according unto thy word —Ps 119:107

In some passages the Bible states that God has seen and regarded the affliction of His people and the afflicted testify to it time and time again:

And Leah conceived, and bare a son, and she called his name Reuben: for she said, Surely the Lord hath looked upon my affliction; now therefore my husband will love me —Genesis 29:32

And the Lord said, I have surely seen the affliction of my people which are in Egypt, and have heard their cry by reason of their taskmasters; for I know their sorrows —Exodus 3:7

And the people believed: and when they heard that the Lord had visited the children of Israel, and that he had looked upon their affliction, then they bowed their heads and worshipped —Exodus 4:31

Nevertheless he regarded their affliction, when he heard their cry —Psalm 106:44

We further learn that God does not despise or abhor the affliction of His people — **For he hath not despised nor abhorred the affliction of the afflicted; neither hath he hid his face from him; but when he cried unto him, he heard — Psalm 22:24**

Assurances are present in their testimonies that their God delivers them from their troubles — **He delivereth the poor**

in his affliction, and openeth their ears in oppression
—Job 36:15

And the afflicted people thou wilt save: but thine eyes are upon the haughty, that thou mayest bring them down. For thou art my lamp, O Lord: and the Lord will lighten my darkness —2 Samuel 22:28-30

The righteous cry, and the Lord heareth, and delivereth them out of all their troubles. The Lord is nigh unto them that are of a broken heart; and saveth such as be of a contrite spirit. Many are the afflictions of the righteous: but the Lord delivereth him out of them all —Psalm 34:17-19

Often where the affliction suffered by God's people is mentioned there is also reference to their God who hears their cry:

So that they cause the cry of the poor to come unto him, and he heareth the cry of the afflicted —Job 34:25 KJV

And when we cried unto the Lord God of our fathers, the Lord heard our voice, and looked on our affliction, and our labour, and our oppression —Deuteronomy 26:7

If, when evil cometh upon us, as the sword, judgment, or pestilence, or famine, we stand before this house, and in thy presence, (for thy name is in this house,) and cry unto thee in our affliction, then thou wilt hear and help —2 Chronicles 20:9

Thou art the Lord the God... And didst see the affliction of our fathers in Egypt, and heardest their cry by the Red sea —Nehemiah 9:7, 9

And said, I cried by reason of mine affliction unto the Lord, and he heard me; out of the belly of hell cried I, and thou heardest my voice —Jonah 2:2

And the angel of the Lord said unto her, Behold, thou art with child, and shalt bear a son, and shalt call his name Ishmael; because the Lord hath heard thy affliction —Genesis 16:11

When searching the Bible for the many passages that refer to affliction I could find only one that stated that God had heard their affliction. It was these words that brought me to the conclusion of the possibility that affliction might have a sound.

Affliction Connected To Music

I continued to look into the meaning of affliction and I noticed a word that was used, "Leannoth"[4] which is a musical term or instruction. Musical instructions are often found in some of the opening clauses of the Psalms. There are twelve terms referring to the musical melodies used in performing the Psalms:

1   Shiggayon

2   Alamoth

3   Sheminith

4   Nehiloth

5   Gittith

6   Shoshanim

7   Mahalath

8   Jonath Elem Rehokim

9   Ayyeleth Hashshahar

10   Al - Tashheth

11   Almoth Labben

12   Eduth

For the most part, when reading the Psalms we tend not to pay much attention to these musical terms. The words are strange and in some cases hard to pronounce so most people skip over them to the main content of the Psalm. However, I have found that sometimes the musical term or instruction contained in the title of the Psalm provides some insight into the tone or mood of the content of the Psalm.

An article on Music in the Nelson Bible Dictionary gives us an insight into importance of music to God's people. In fact music was part of everyday life for the ancient Hebrew people. It was a part of family merrymaking, such as the homecoming party for the prodigal son (Luke 15:25).

Music welcomed heroes and celebrated victories. Miriam and other women sang, danced, and played tambourines when the Israelites miraculously escaped the Egyptians (Exodus 15:20), and the Song of Moses in Exodus 15 is the earliest recorded song in the Bible. Jephthah's daughter greeted him with tambourines to celebrate his victory over the Ammonites (Judges 11:34). David's triumph over Goliath the Philistine inspired musical celebrations (1 Samuel 18:6-7).

Music was used in making war and crowning kings (Judges 7:18-20; 1 Kings 1:39-40; 2 Chronicles 20:28). Wartime music-making, on the surface, seemed like little more than making noise, but was effective when we take into consideration the events surrounding the fall of the Walls of Jericho (Joshua 6).

There was music for banquets and feasts (Isaiah 5:12; 24:8-9) and royal courts and harems (Ecclesiastes 2:8). The Bible gives examples of occupational songs (Jeremiah 31:4-5), dirges and laments (Matthew 9:23), and cultic chants (Exodus 28:34-35; Joshua 6:4-20).

Apparently, the Jews were very musical people. Included in the tribute that King Hezekiah of Judah paid to the Assyrian king, Sennacherib, were male and female Judean musicians and singers (according to the Tyndale Biblical Archaeology Lecture, 1984 — Sennacherib's Attack on Hezekiah). Psalm 137 narrates that the Babylonians demanded "songs of Zion" from the Israelites while they were in captivity (v. 3). During the period between the Old and New testaments, Strabo,[5] a Greek geographer and historian, called the female singers of Palestine the most musical in the world.

In the Old Testament, we see that Jubal was "the father of all those who play the harp and flute" (Genesis 4:21) but professional musicians do not appear in the Bible before David's time. Even before professional musicians became the norm during David's reign, the concept of court musicians did exist. The young David was called to soothe Saul with music (1 Samuel 16:16-23). In this sense David was a minstrel (2 Kings 3:15) — a player of stringed instruments.

The New Testament minstrels (Matthew 9:23) were flute-players employed as professional mourners. The transition from spontaneous music to professional male musicians chiefly associated with organised religion was a natural one. Israel's neighbours, Assyria and Egypt, were also known for their professional musicians who were an integral part of everyday life. In spite of God's command to avoid other cultures, Israel was nevertheless strongly influenced by them — in music as well as religious practices.

Exactly how music was used in the tabernacle and Temple services is not known. But scholars are certain that it accompanied sacrificial rites. Sacrificial music was forbidden after the Romans destroyed the Temple in 70 AD. The Levites, Temple assistants responsible for the music, seem to have kept this part of the service a secret.
David introduced music into the sanctuary worship and his son and successor, Solomon later retained it after the Temple was built (2 Samuel 6:5; 1 Kings 10:12). Music must have been considered an important part of the service, since Hezekiah and Josiah, the two kings of Judah responsible for the reforms of the Kingdom worship practices, saw to it that music was included in the reformation (2 Chronicles 29:25; 35:15).

Asaph, Heman, and Jeduthun (Ethan) helped David set up the sanctuary worship. Asaph headed a choir of singers and musicians who were stationed before the Ark of the Covenant in Jerusalem. Heman and Jeduthun had similar choirs at the old Tabernacle at Gibeon (1 Chronicles 16:4-6, 39-42). These choirs had 4,000 members (1 Chronicles 23:5); 288 of these were trained musicians who directed the lesser-skilled musicians (1 Chronicles 25:7-8). All the musicians were divided into 24 courses (teams), each containing 12 skilled musicians. An orchestra consisting of stringed instruments (harps and lyres) and cymbals accompanied the singers (1 Chronicles 15:19-21).

The New Testament contains little information about music. But it does give some additional hymns to add to the Old Testament hymns — Those of Mary (Luke 1:46-55) and Zacharias (Luke 1:68-79) — the Magnificat (Song of Mary) and the Benedictus (Song of Zacharias) respectively. Early Christians sang Hebrew songs accompanied by music (2 Chronicles 29:27-28).

The Apostle Paul refers to "Psalms and hymns and spiritual songs" (Ephesians 5:19; Col 3:16). Matthew 26:30 records that Christ and His disciples sang a hymn after the Passover supper, probably the second half of the Hallel, or Psalm 115-118.

> There is a song or a unique sound that only comes from the afflicted

Our greatest clue to Hebrew music lies in the Book of Psalms, the earliest existing hymnbook. As hymns, these individual Psalms were suitable for chanting and singing in the worship of God. The Bible gives a glimpse of musical terminology in the headings of the Psalms which appear in the Hebrew language, the language in which the

Old Testament was originally written. Their meanings, however, are, to a large extent, obscure. These meanings were apparently lost as early as 250 BC, the approximate date of the Greek translation of the Old Testament.

Some of the categories of the Psalm headings include the following: "Mizmor" from Psalm 87 seems to mean "to play, sing"; "Maschil" from Psalm 78 may indicate a meditation; "Alamoth" from Psalm 46 may mean "for the flutes" or for soprano voices; "Sheminith from Psalm 6; Psalm 12 suggests a melodic pattern, perhaps an octave lower than "Alamoth" and, therefore, tenor or even bass. The New King James Version translates, "on an eight-stringed harp." "Neginoth from Psalms 4; 6; 54; 55; 61; 67; 76) is translated "stringed instruments". "Shiggaion" from Psalm 7, possibly meaning a "Psalm of lamentation". "Mahalath from Psalm 53, probably meaning "a choreographic direction."

I should point out that all of the meanings of these terms are speculative with little upon which to base a firm opinion. The musical term that started me on this train of thought as I mentioned before was "Leannoth". In Psalm 88 "Mahalath" is coupled with "Leannoth" and has had some varied and uncertain meaning but is generally interpreted as "for singing antiphonally" and "concerning sickness, to be sung" i.e., perhaps, to be sung in sickness.

The addition of "Leannoth" from the root word, *aanah* meaning "to afflict" could bring us to the conclusion that Psalm 88 is a song that expresses "concerning the sickness of affliction." Praise songs were considered the comfort of the afflicted. Psalm 88 is described as one of the gloomiest of all the Psalms. The "maschil" or instruction is that the afflicted should pour out their grief to God.

O Jehovah, God of my salvation, I have wept before you day and night. Now hear my prayers; oh, listen to my cry, for my life is full of troubles, and death draws near —Psalm 88:1-3 (The Living Bible).

Further descriptions give direction that the Psalm should be sung in a slow pensive tone (moestoso).

Some scholars and translators have connected the term "Leannoth" with the Hebrew word for "sick" and further translations surmise the heading to be the direction of "a sad tune", or perhaps a tune that begins with "the Illness of so and so…" or "the song of the afflicted." It seems that psalmist was experiencing a severe and oppressive time of affliction. This seems to be confirmed by the words of the Psalm depicted in the verses below:

A Song or Psalm for the sons of Ko'-rah, to the chief Musician upon Mahalath Leannoth, Maschil of Heman the Ezrahite.

Mine eye mourneth by reason of affliction: Lord, I have called daily upon thee, I have stretched out my hands unto thee—Verse 9

I am afflicted and ready to die from my youth up: while I suffer thy terrors I am distracted. Thy fierce wrath goeth over me; thy terrors have cut me off. They came round about me daily like water; they compassed me about together. Lover and friend hast thou put far from me, and mine acquaintance into darkness—Verses 15-18

Perhaps there is song or a unique sound that only comes from the afflicted. It could be that, unbeknown to us, when we are suffering our sound changes on so many levels.

What
Is Sound?

According to The Oxford English Dictionary Sound is defined as 'vibrations that travel through the air or another medium and can be heard when they reach a person's or animal's ear.'[6]

Other reference sources define sound in other ways using various degrees of complexity. When investigating sound I realised how intentional God was when He gave us ears! Also, He didn't just give us the ability to hear but also to create sounds and the awesome and wonderful thing about sound is that God responds to the sounds we make.

If you take time to consider how complex and integral sound is, it is impossible to visualise it as a random phenomenon. Sound is so much more and we should be so grateful and really appreciate how valuable it is. Before I move forward with the deep spiritual perspective of sound and what it means to us as Christians I have included some factual information on sound that I feel it is important to know. One reference source defines sound as an audible mechanical wave propagating through matter, or the perception of such waves by the brain.[7]

Another source states that sound waves are among the most basic and common sound waves. There are two types of sound waves, which are transverse and longitudinal waves. Transverse waves are typically produced by electromagnetic devices and objects, such as light, radio and television. Sound can also exist as longitudinal waves, which are produced by mechanical vibrations in machinery and industrial equipment.[8]

According to Wikipedia,[9] in physics, sound is a vibration that propagates as a typically audible mechanical wave of pressure and displacement, through a transmission medium such as air or water. In physiology and psychology, sound is the reception of such waves and their perception by the brain. Humans can hear sound waves with frequencies between about 20 Hz and 20 kHz.

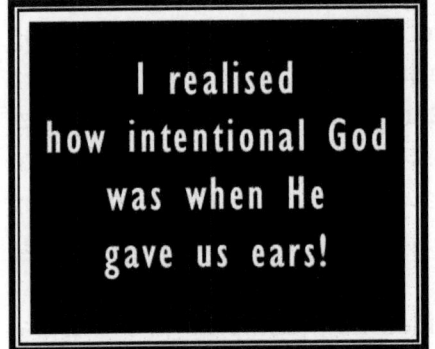

I realised how intentional God was when He gave us ears!

Sound above 20 kHz is ultrasound and below 20 Hz is infrasound. In air at standard temperature and pressure, the corresponding wavelengths of sound waves range from 17 metres to 17 millimetres. Animals have different hearing ranges.

As a signal perceived by one of the major senses, sound is used by many species for detecting danger, navigation, predation, and communication. Earth's atmosphere, water, and virtually any physical phenomenon, such as fire, rain, wind, ocean surf, or earthquake, produces (and is characterised by) its unique sounds. Many species, such as frogs, birds, marine and terrestrial mammals, have also developed special organs to produce sound. In some species, these produce song and speech.

Furthermore, humans have developed culture and technology (such as music, telephone and radio) that allows us to generate, record, transmit, and broadcast sound. There are six experimentally separable ways in which sound waves are analysed. They are: pitch, duration, loudness, timbre, sonic texture and spatial location.

Pitch is perceived as how "low" or "high" a sound is and represents the cyclic, repetitive nature of the vibrations that make up sound. For simple sounds, pitch relates to the frequency of the slowest vibration in the sound (called the fundamental harmonic). In the case of complex sounds, pitch perception can vary. Sometimes individuals identify different pitches for the same sound, based on their personal experience of particular sound patterns.

Duration is perceived as how "long" or "short" a sound is and relates to onset and offset signals created by nerve responses to sounds. The duration of a sound usually lasts from the time the sound is first noticed until the sound is identified as having changed or ceased. Sometimes this is not directly related to the physical duration of a sound.

Loudness is perceived as how "loud" or "soft" a sound is and relates to the totalled number of auditory nerve stimulations over short cyclic time periods. This means that at short durations, a very short sound can sound softer than a longer sound even though they are presented at the same intensity level. Louder signals create a greater 'push' on the Basilar Membrane (situated in the inner ear) and thus stimulate more nerves, creating a stronger loudness signal. A more complex signal also creates more nerve firings and so sounds louder.

Timbre is perceived as the quality of different sounds (e.g. the thud of a fallen rock, the whir of a drill, the tone of a musical instrument or the quality of a voice) and represents the pre-conscious allocation of a sonic identity to a sound (e.g. "It's my mother's voice!").

Sonic texture relates to the number of sound sources and the interaction between them. The word 'texture', in this context, relates to the cognitive separation of auditory objects. In music, texture is often referred to as the difference between unison, polyphony and homophony, but it can also relate (for example) to a busy cafe; a sound which might be referred to as 'cacophony'. However texture refers to more than this.

The texture of an orchestral piece is very different to the texture of a brass quartet because of the different numbers of players. The texture of a market place is very different to a school hall because of the differences in the various sound sources.

Spatial location represents the cognitive placement of a

sound in an environmental context; including the placement of a sound on both the horizontal and vertical plane, the distance from the sound source and the characteristics of the sonic environment. In a thick texture, it is possible to identify multiple sound sources using a combination of spatial location and timbre identification. It is the main reason why we can pick the sound of an oboe in an orchestra and the words of a single person in a crowded room.[10] In short, sound is simply amazing!

More To Sound Than Meets The Ear!

Since the dawn of time, mankind has used sound to receive information from the environment to communicate with each other and to heal and transform. Almost all ancient cultures and indigenous people believed, and still believe, that sound is the creative, generative force which brought the Universe into being.

In the New Testament John 1:1 states **"In the Beginning was the Word, and the Word was with God, and the Word was God"** "The Word" quite clearly refers to sound, which is the God-force or creative force (Elohim) of the Universe. Everything in the Universe is made up of Atoms.[11]

Every atom consists of a nucleus (neutrons and protons) and electrons which spin rapidly around the nucleus. The number of each of these particles differs according to the nature of the matter. The

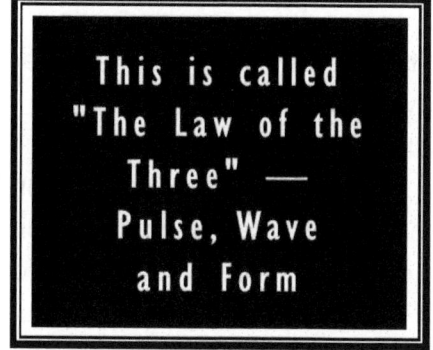

This is called "The Law of the Three" — Pulse, Wave and Form

spinning motion of the electrons initiates a pulse, which

creates a wave, and this wave we perceive with our human perception, as form, or matter. Whenever Pulse, Wave and Form, are present there is sound. This is called "The Law of the Three".[12]

This is an interesting point when we consider how many significant 'threes' can be found in general and also throughout the Bible. One that comes to mind straightaway is the presence of the Deity, the triune nature of God: Father, Son and Holy Spirit — termed by some as the Trinity and by others as the Godhead. Also, God's attributes are generally cited as: omniscience, omnipresence, and omnipotence. On further research I've discovered that there seems to be a purposeful and notable presence of 'threes' almost wherever you look.

Diagram of an atom

'Threes' are found in many places in the human body: 3 layers of skin — the epidermis, dermis and hypodermis; 3 bones in the middle ear — the incus, malleus and stapes; 3 parts to the ear — the outer, middle and the inner; 3 semi-circular canals in the inner ear; 3 intrinsic muscles of the tongue — longitudinal, vertical and transverse; 3 types of deciduous teeth — incisors, canine and molars; 3 layers of dentition in the teeth — enamel, dentin and pulp; 3 general layers of the eye — retinal, choroidal/ciliary body and scleral/corneal; 3 colour receptors in the cone cells of the eye — red, blue and yellow; 3 cerebral arteries in the brain — anterior, middle and posterior; 3 parts of the stomach — fundus, body and pylorus; 3 smooth muscle layers of the stomach — oblique, longitudinal and circular; 3 parts of the small intestine — duodenum, jejunum and ileum; 3 parts of large intestine — ascending, transverse and descending;

In sacred Scripture the number 3 represents that which is solid, real, substantial, and something in its completeness. This number usually indicates something of importance or significance in God's plan of salvation by identifying an important event in Salvation History. This number operates as a "sign-post" in Scripture study for the reader to "pay attention" to the significance of the next event.[13]

In the Old Testament: It is the first of the 4 perfect numbers which are 3 (divine perfection); 7 (spiritual perfection); 10 (ordinal perfection); and 12 (governmental perfection). There were 3 Patriarchs of the children of Israel: Abraham, Isaac and Jacob/Israel. There are 3 verses in the Priestly Blessing in which the Tetragrammaton, YHWH, God's holy covenant name, appears 3 times (Numbers 6:24-26).

The angelic Seraphim cry 3 times, "HOLY, HOLY, HOLY" (Isaiah 6:3 and Revelation 4:8). After the Great Flood, mankind descended from the 3 sons of Noah, Shem, Ham, and Japheth (Genesis 10:1-32). 3 men (angels) announced to Abraham that his barren wife, Sarah would bear a son (Genesis 18:14). Abraham was commanded to sacrifice his son after a 3-day journey to Mount Moriah (Genesis 22:1-4). Baby Moses was hidden by his mother for 3 months (Exodus 2:1). Moses requested that Pharaoh let him take his people on a 3 day journey into the wilderness to offer sacrifices to their God (Exodus 3:18).

There are 3 attributes of God that are referred to in Exodus 33:18-19: 'hen', 'rachum', and 'hesed' (gracious, compassionate/merciful, and loving kindness).

Out of the 7 Holy Feasts of the Sinai Covenant, 3 are pilgrim feasts in which every man 13 years or older must present himself before God at the Temple in Jerusalem. This command is repeated 3 times in Scripture (Exodus 23:14-17; 34:18-23; Deuteronomy 16:16). Jonah was in the belly of the whale for 3 days and 3 nights (Jonah 1:17). Jonah took a 3 day journey across the city of Nineveh (Jonah 3:3). Esther came before king on the third day and found favour (Esther 5:1-2). There were 3 main parts to the Tabernacles — the Outer Court, Inner Court and Most Holy Place (Exodus 24-27).

> Paul saw visions and revelations of the third heaven

In the New Testament: Jesus' ministry lasted 3 years. Jesus prayed 3 times in the Garden of Gethsemane before His arrest (Matthew 26:36-44). Jesus was crucified at the

3rd hour and died at the 9th hour (multiple of 3) (Mark 15:25). There were 3 hours of darkness that covered the land while Jesus was dying, from the 6th hour to the 9th hour (Matthew 27:44-45). Mary stayed with Elizabeth for about 3 months when she was pregnant (Luke 1:56). Jesus was missing for 3 days when He was 12 years old (Luke 2:46). Jesus took 3 disciples with Him up to the Mount of Transfiguration — Peter, James, and John (Matthew 17). Jesus arose from the dead on the third day (Matthew 16:21, Acts 10:40).

Saul was blinded for 3 days (Acts 9:9). The theological virtues are stated as Faith, Hope, and Charity (1 Corinthians 13:13). The heavenly Jerusalem has 3 gates on each of its four sides (Revelation 21:13). 3 is also recognised as the number of the Holy Spirit — The third person of the Trinity. Paul saw visions and revelations of the third heaven (2 Corinthians 12:1-2).

From a general perspective, there are 3 divisions of time — Past, Present and Future. In school we're taught that there are 3 persons in grammar; the category "First person" refers to the speaker himself or a group that includes the speaker (i.e., I, me, we and us). "Second person" refers to the speaker's audience (i.e., you). "Third person" refers to everybody else (e.g., he, him, she, her, it, they, them), including all other nouns. Thought, Word and Deed complete the sum of human capacity. So as we can see the number three is important.

Let's get back to sound waves and these three areas —

Pulse, Wave and Form. All matter is sound, and emits sound, although these sounds are mostly beyond our limited physical sense of hearing. So, although we may not be able to physically hear certain sounds, God can.

I believe that our affliction has a sound that others can't hear but God can. So, when everyone dismisses you as neurotic and as an imbalanced person with fanciful issues or tells you that you are too much of a problem or treats you like you're not worth the time of day. Making you feel worthless and of no use in this earth. When your suffering and times of affliction seem unending and unbearable. Remember that, your affliction has a sound that God, if no one else, will pay attention to.

> Scientific research shows that we are in constant motion or vibration

This makes sense when you consider the fact that our physical bodies, are resonant or vibrating, electromagnetic fields, as are our auras, both generated by the atoms of which we consist. An aura,[14] in simple terms is the 'distinctive atmosphere or quality that seems to surround and be generated by a person, thing, or place'. I should point out that although other religions and agencies put emphasis or base teachings on the effect, power, psychic, colour or energy of auras, I am only referring to the aura in its simplest and basic sense and in relation to the vibrations of our bodies.

Scientific research has shown that we are in constant motion or vibration.[15] Every molecule, cell, tissue, organ, gland, bone and liquid in our bodies has its own specific rate of vibration. Humans, like all known things in the universe, are in constant motion. However, aside from obvious movements of the various external body parts and locomotion, humans are in motion in a variety of ways which are more difficult to perceive. Many of these "imperceptible motions" are only perceivable with the help of special tools and careful observation.

The larger scales of "imperceptible motions" are difficult for humans to perceive for two reasons: 1) Newton's laws of motion[16] (particularly inertia) which prevent humans from feeling motions of a mass to which they are connected, and 2) the lack of an obvious frame of reference which would allow individuals to easily see that they are moving. The smaller scales of these motions are too small for humans to sense. We are, however, aware of this motion in some cases even we are unable to see it.

The human heart is constantly contracting to move blood throughout the body. Through larger veins and arteries in the body, blood has been found to travel at approximately 0.33 metres per second. Though considerable variation exists, and peak flows in the venae cavae (veins) have been found between 0.1 meters per second and 0.45 metres per second.

The smooth muscles of hollow internal organs are moving. The most familiar would be peristalsis which is where digested food is forced throughout the digestive tract. Though different foods travel through the body at varying rates, the average speed through the human small intestine is 2.16 metres per hour.

The human lymphatic system is constantly moving excess fluids, lipids, and immune system related products around the body. The lymph fluid has been found to move through a lymph capillary of the skin at approximately 0.0000097 metres per second.

According to the Laws of Thermodynamics[17] all particles of matter are in constant random motion. Thus the molecules and atoms which make up the human body are vibrating, colliding, and moving. This motion can be detected as temperature; higher temperatures, which represent greater kinetic energy in the particles, feel warm to humans whom sense the thermal energy transferring from the object being touched to their nerves. Similarly, when lower temperature objects are touched, the senses perceive the transfer of heat away from the body as feeling cold.

In relation to sound it is understood that typically some sound is audible at any given moment. When the vibration of these sound waves reaches the ear drum it moves in response and allows the sense of hearing. So in summary, we are generally oblivious to the constant motion and vibration of the integral parts of our bodies.

It follows then that we would also not be aware when our

affliction or illness or condition is in motion or vibrating or making sound. So, I suppose it's not too farfetched for me to believe that in my deepest and darkest moments when I am unable to voice my distress, that my affliction speaks for me.

The Science Of Cymatics

As I looked more closely at sound I discovered that there are so many interesting facets to sound that left me more in awe of our Creator God than ever before. It cemented and made it more concrete for me that everything that our Jehovah God does is truly purposeful and intended.

For the Lord of hosts hath purposed, and who shall disannul it? and his hand is stretched out, and who shall turn it back? —Isaiah 14:27

Sound vibration patterns on metal plate

The Science of Cymatics[18] most visually demonstrates the ways that sound shapes or affects matter. Cymatics is derived from the Greek: κῦμα (kuma), meaning "wave". Cymatics was "discovered" by the Swiss physician and natural scientist Doctor Hans Jenny.[19] He coined the term 'Cymatics' to describe acoustic effects of sound wave phenomena.

In 1967, Jenny published the first volume of "Cymatics: The Study of Wave Phenomena". His second volume was published in 1972, the year that he died. This book was a written and photographic documentation of the effects of sound waves and how they affect us. He was not the only one to notice this significant phenomenon. Ernst Chladni[20] was a German physicist and musician. He is sometimes referred to as the Father of Acoustics.

His research and experiments showed that fine powders, sand and iron filings, when placed on a flat metal plate and vibrated with soundwaves, arranged themselves into intricate patterns. The various substances concentrated themselves in the troughs of the soundwaves, thus highlighting the areas where the sound was most dense. These wonderful patterns are also known as Chladni Figures.[21] These experiments he did were similar to those carried out earlier by Galileo[22] around 1630 and by Robert Hooke[23] in 1680. They were later perfected

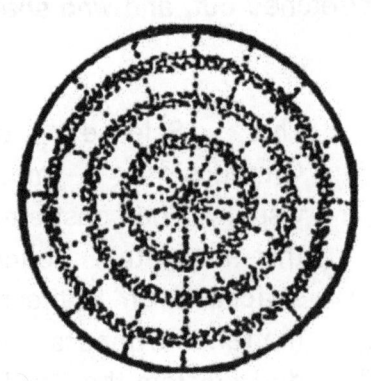

Example of Chladni Figure

by Chladni, who introduced them systematically in 1787 in his book titled Entdeckungen über die Theorie des Klanges ("Discoveries in the Theory of Sound") which was first published in 1787.

Later, Hans Jenny would conduct a similar experiment where he spread quartz sand onto a black drum membrane 60 cm in diameter. The membrane was caused to vibrate by singing loudly through a cardboard pipe, and the sand produced symmetrical Chladni patterns. Low tones resulted in rather simple and clear pictures, while higher tones formed more complex structures.

According to Jenny, he observed that these structures were similar to the structure of the mandala[24] and other forms naturally recurring in nature. The word "mandala" is from the classical Indian language of Sanskrit, loosely translated to mean "circle".

In that culture the mandala is seen as far more than a simple shape. It represents wholeness, and is seen as a model for the organisational structure of life itself — a cosmic diagram that reminds us of our relation to the infinite, the world that extends both beyond and within our

Examples of circles in nature

bodies and minds. The mandala is then seen to appear in all aspects of life: the celestial circles we call earth, sun, and moon, as well as conceptual circles of friends, family, and community. This integrated view of the world represented by the mandala, while long embraced by some Eastern religions, has now begun to emerge in Western religious and secular cultures.

Now, I should point out that I do not endorse the religious beliefs or spiritual practices born from a revering viewpoint and/or deistical perception of the mandala. However, I cannot negate the fact that throughout creation the 'circle' is a naturally occurring shape that is seen over and over again — the moon, the sun, the planets, shells, flowers, fruit, etc. which brings me right back to the purposefulness of Jehovah God. So, for me, personally, this would be the only emphasis that I would make concerning mandala.

On another note, in my research I found out that the New Age movement has been quick to claim that Cymatics has special healing properties. It has been proposed that sound waves generating particular patterns may stimulate healing, although this does not appear to be related to Cymatics but rather its function of acoustics. Generally, it is believed that there is no medical evidence of this phenomenon.

This viewpoint is due to, what some see as, the spurious claims by New Age healers. Cymatics is very much regarded as pseudoscience by the scientific community at large, who see the phenomenon as showing nothing more than the information displayed on an oscilloscope.

I believe this area of science, for the most part, shows us how amazing and purposeful Elohim, our creator God is. The science of Cymatics is just one of many areas that you can see God's omniscience at work. There have been remarkable developments since Chladni's vibrating plates. Researchers and scientists have developed other ways to observe sound waves and their effect on us and matter in general. Over the last 2 decades the process in which the effects of sound wave vibrations can be made visible has advanced quite a lot.

The CymaScope[25] is an instrument developed by English acoustics engineer John Stuart Reid and design engineer Erik Larson.[26] The CymaScope works by directing the vibrations of different sound frequencies toward a surface of a liquid. In other words sonic (sound) vibrations are imprinted on 'ultra-pure water'. The geometric vibrations in the water produce images and make sound visible. The patterns are digitally captured using a digital camera. The type of geometry represented by many Cymatics images contains reoccurring themes like spheres, hexagons and spirals.

It has also been discovered by scientists at cymascope.com, that the notes of a piano make geometric patterns. Each note forms a unique geometric shape. They have categorised the notes into octaves outlined on their CymaPiano.[27] Now, the developers and creatives at CymaScope have also released their Cymascope App for iPad and iPhone.[28] The CymaScope app is the world's first app to make the geometry of piano sounds and music visible. The imagery you will see is not a computer simulation; all the beautiful imagery in the app was created on a physical CymaScope then stored in digital memory for patrons to enjoy. The Music Made Visible App is a breakthrough in providing an accessible tool showcasing this technology for use in a variety of applications.

If one tone can create these imprints, imagine the effect that the amalgamation of harsh or unnatural sounds can have on our bodies. The theory is that the vibrational geometry of nature can bring us back into balance while the noise pollution and increasing electromagnetic fields around us can throw us off or in a worst-case scenario cause disease.

I've realised that everything is connected when we start to look at the basic essence of vibration. Despite the fact that there are some circles of thought who have written-off or disregard the possibility of Cymatics (vibration of sound waves at certain frequencies) being connected to healing, it is generally agreed beyond a shadow of a doubt that sound anywhere near the human body will create a physical change within the body. This change may be only temporary but in some circles it is termed by the phrase, 'a moment of healing'. I leave you to draw your own conclusions.

Sound Therapy– Science Or Myth?

As I looked more into sound and how it affects us, I came across a form of therapy called Sound Therapy. According to a health and wellbeing article on the Guardian website (dated 6th July 2008),[29] Sound therapists believe that our bodies contain 'energy frequencies' and that sonic or sound frequencies can be used to re-attune these energies when they go off key. This can be done by exposing the body to certain frequencies. Whether it's Mozart or Motown, music affects us all in different ways

In general, responses to music are able to be observed.[30] It has been proven that music influences us in both good and bad ways. These effects are instant and long lasting. Music is thought to link all of the emotional, spiritual, and physical elements of the universe.

Music can also be used to change a person's mood, and has been found to cause similar physical responses in many different people simultaneously. Music also has the ability to strengthen or weaken emotions.

When looking at responses to music, rhythm is also an important aspect of music which warrants further study.

There are two responses to rhythm. These responses are hard to separate because they are related, and one cannot exist without the other. These responses are (1) the actual hearing of the rhythm and (2) the physical response to the rhythm.

There is proof that music influences us in both good and bad ways

I found out that Rhythm actually organises our physical movements and is very much related to the human body. For example, the body contains rhythms in the heartbeat as we go about our daily routines, while we are walking, during our breathing, etc.

Another example I can give of how rhythm orders our movement is with an autistic boy who could not tie his shoelaces. He learned how on the second try when the task of tying his shoelaces was put to a song. The rhythm helped organise his physical movements in time.

Also early missionaries to Africa thought that the natives had bad rhythm. The missionaries said that when the natives played on their drums it sounded like they were not beating in time. However, it was later discovered that they were beating out complex polyrhythmic beats such as 2 against 3, 3 against 4, and 2 against 3 and 5, etc. These beats were too advanced for the missionaries to follow.

Responses to music are easy to be detected in the human body. Classical music from the Baroque Period has been seen to show marked responses in the body. The Baroque Period is known for its style of Western European art music composed from about 1600 to 1750. Composers of this era include Johann Sebastian Bach, Antonio Vivaldi, George Frederick Handel, Claudio Monteverdi, Henry Purcell and others that you may be familiar with. Baroque style music causes the heart beat and pulse rate to relax to the beat of the music. As the body becomes relaxed and alert, the mind is able to concentrate more easily.

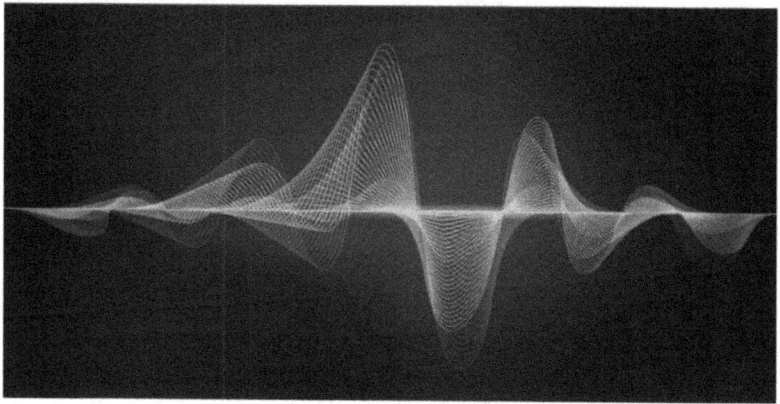

Example of Sound Wave Pattern

Furthermore, it has been observed that Baroque Music decreases blood pressure and enhances the ability to learn.

In general, music affects the amplitude and frequency of brainwaves. This can be measured using an encephalogram. Music also affects breathing rate and electrical resistance of the skin. It has also been found that certain types of music can cause a biochemical response resulting in the release of a neurotransmitter called Norepinephrine which causes the pupils to dilate, a raise in blood pressure and also increased heart rate.

The key component of music that makes it beneficial is order. The order of the music from the Baroque and Classical Periods causes the brain to respond in special ways. This order includes repetition and changes, certain patterns of rhythm, and pitch and mood contrasts. One key ingredient to the order of music from the Baroque and Classical Periods is math. This is realised by the body and the human mind performs better when listening to this ordered music.

One suggested example of the power of order in music is King George I of England. King George had problems with memory loss and stress management. He read the story of King Saul in the Bible (1 Samuel 16:23) and concluded that his problems were comparable to those experienced by King Saul. King George noted that King Saul overcame his 'problems' by using special music. With this story in mind King George asked George Frederick Handel to write some special music for him that would help him in the same way that music helped Saul. Some say that Handel wrote his Water Music for this purpose.

Another key to the order in music is the music being the same and different. The brain works by looking at different pieces of information and deciding if they are different or the same. This is done in music of the Baroque and

Classical periods by playing a theme and then repeating or changing the theme. The repetition is only done once. More than one repetition causes the music to become displeasing, and also causes a person to either enter a state of sub-conscious thinking or a state of anger.

Dr Michael Ballam, a renowned professor of music, an accomplished operatic singer, pianist and oboist, pointed out that, "The human mind shuts down after three or four repetitions of a rhythm, or a melody, or a harmonic progression." Furthermore, excessive repetition causes people to release control of their thoughts. Rhythmic repetition is often used by people who are trying to push certain ethics in their music.

An Australian physician and psychiatrist, Dr John Diamond, found a direct link between muscle strength/weakness and music. He discovered that all of the muscles in the entire body go weak when subjected to the "stopped anapestic beat" of music from hard rock musicians such as Led Zeppelin, Alice Cooper, Queen, Janis Joplin and others.

Dr Diamond also found another effect of the anapestic beat. He called it a "switching" of the brain. Dr Diamond said this switching occurs when the actual symmetry between both of the cerebral hemispheres is destroyed causing alarm in the body along with lessened work performance, learning and behaviour problems in children, and a "general malaise in adults."

In addition to harmful, irregular beats in rock music, shrill frequencies prove to also be harmful to the body. Bob Larson, a Christian minister, evangelist and former rock musician, remembers that in the 1970's teens would bring raw eggs to a rock concert and put them on the front of the stage. The eggs would be 'hard boiled by the music' before the end of the concert and could be eaten.

Dr. Earl W. Flosdorf and Dr. Leslie A. Chambers showed that proteins in a liquid medium were coagulated when subjected to piercing high-pitched sounds. We can see that music definitely has an effect on the human body and in turn the human body responds. Let's get back to Sound Therapy and its possible uses.

On a fundamental level, music is just organised sound. Sound Therapy deconstructs music into pure sound, harnessing the knowledge that sound can have a powerful effect on our emotions. Sound therapists believe that we are all made up of different energy frequencies. They use sound frequencies to interact with these, thus attempting to rebalance the body's energy.

Practitioners have documented clinical case studies that demonstrate the positive effect of Sound Therapy, but it is a relatively new practice in the UK, so many of the claims are under-researched and unsubstantiated. However, a study conducted by the British Academy of Sound Therapy (BAST)[31] found that 95% of clients suffering from stress-related disorders felt an increased state of calm following treatment (although, of course, I know that their findings would not be regarded as unbiased research!)

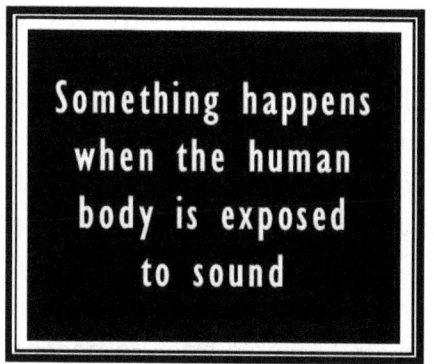

Something happens when the human body is exposed to sound

Another preliminary study conducted by BAST measured the effects of Sound Therapy on the autonomous nervous system (ANS). Clients were connected to a machine that monitored stress responses (much like a lie detector). Each client demonstrated an overall decrease in arousal of the ANS compared to the control group, who were lying down relaxing. This study suggests that Sound Therapy has a deeply calming effect on stressed-out clients. Sound has been used as a healing or calming tool for thousands of years. Himalayan singing bowls (standing bells that "sing") have been used throughout Asia for thousands of years in prayer and meditation, and are now used to promote relaxation and wellbeing.

Sound Therapy was formally introduced to the UK in 2000 with the establishment of BAST. Sound Therapy is a complementary medicine designed to work alongside orthodox medicine. Sound Therapy is said to help not only physical illness, but also help balance the emotions and quieten a busy mind. Most people feel calm and relaxed following Sound Therapy treatment.

While it is understandable that Sound Therapy is viewed with some scepticism I did find some information on the subject of low-amplitude high-frequency sound used in bone fracture healing.[32] Fracture healing involves a complex interplay of cellular processes, culminating in bridging of a fracture gap with bone. Fracture healing can be compromised by numerous exogenous and endogenous patient factors, and intense research is currently going on to identify modalities that can increase the likelihood of successful healing. Low-Intensity Pulsed Ultrasound (LIPUS) has been proposed as a modality that may have a benefit for increasing reliable fracture healing as well as perhaps increasing the rate of fracture healing.

It seems to me that there is some credibility to the positive effect of sound on the human body. You may not wish to use terms like 'Sound Therapy' or 'energy' or 'frequencies' but I hope you are realising that something definitely happens when the human body is exposed to sound.

What I have also realised in my investigations into sound is that we are affected differently by different types of sound. It follows then that the sounds we make, whether they can be heard by the human ear or not, will be different. People will respond differently when sustaining the same injury based on how they are affected by it. One might scream, another may cry and another may howl. They may have sustained the same injury but they will respond differently.

So perhaps I can say that my affliction will sound different to your affliction but it definitely does have a sound and I believe that this is important as we hold on to the belief that the Lord will deliver us from our afflictions. In fact the Bible states that the righteous one suffers many afflictions but God delivers him out of them all (Psalm 34:19). So then I have this reassurance that before I even begin to cry or howl or moan or groan my affliction has already called out or cried out to God; which means I could come to the conclusion that by the time I have released my tears and have said a few prayers, the Lord has already released my deliverance.

The Scripture that comes to mind and takes on a deeper meaning is Isaiah 65:24 — **And it shall come to pass, that before they call, I will answer; and while they are yet speaking, I will hear.** Before I open my mouth the Lord has promised that He will answer. The New Living Translation puts it this way **I will answer them before they even call to me. While they are still talking about their needs, I will go ahead and answer their prayers!**

Is it possible that before I can formulate my words and work out my prayer strategy to God that my affliction has already started making sounds? Could it be possible that before I start crying out to God that my affliction has already begun communicating in its own way? I believe if Hagar was here she would say a resounding and unquestionable Yes!

Sympathetic Resonance

From what I have been able to determine Sound Therapy seems to be generally based on the principle of "sympathetic resonance".[33] Resonance is the vibratory rate of an object, and sympathetic resonance is when one vibrating object causes another to vibrate in harmony with it, or match its rate of vibration. According to a Wikipedia article on the subject sympathetic resonance or sympathetic vibration is a harmonic phenomenon

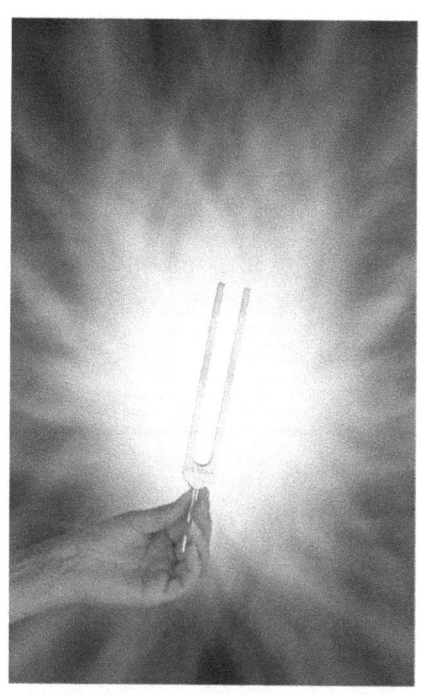

Artist's depiction of tuning fork with sound waves

wherein a formerly passive string or vibratory body responds to external vibrations to which it has a harmonic likeness. The classic example is demonstrated with two similar tuning-forks of which one is mounted on a wooden box. If the other one is struck and then placed on the box, then muted, the un-struck mounted fork will be heard. In a similar way, strings will respond to the external vibrations of a tuning-fork when sufficient harmonic relations exist between the respective vibratory modes.

The principle of sympathetic resonance has been applied in musical instruments from many cultures and eras. There is a basic principle at work on instruments with many undamped strings, such as harps, guitars and pianos with the dampers raised.

The property of sympathetic vibration is encountered in its direct form in room acoustics in the rattling of window panes, light shades and movable panels in the presence of very loud sounds, such as may occasionally be produced by a full pipe organ.

Sympathetic Resonance:
The voice of
the opera singer
shatters the glass

So, if sympathetic resonance is dependent on one vibrating object causing another to vibrate, then when we sing together in our times of affliction, it could be seen as another form of sympathetic resonance or "leannoth (to sing together by course)". In other words, our voices come together in agreement. Our voices produce harmonious vibrations. A visible example of this in the natural is demonstrated when an opera singer breaks a glass with her voice or as stated previously, how passing vehicles may rattle the furniture.

People are amazed when an opera singer breaks a crystal glass with the simple power of her voice.[34] The science behind it is worth mentioning. First of all, the glass used must be crystal. A glass has a natural resonance, a frequency at which it will vibrate easily but crystal resonates at one particular harmonic frequency. You can test whether the glass is suitable by getting a crystal wineglass and dipping your finger in water, then rubbing it gently around the rim of the glass. Your finger will vibrate on the glass, and once you get it right and consistent, the glass will 'hum'.

Another example of resonance can be demonstrated using a narrow mouthed glass bottle; if you blow across the top of a bottle you might get a note. In this case the air in the bottle neck is resonating against the 'spring' provided by the air in the main body of the bottle. In the case of the rubbing your finger around the rim of the glass, the glass hums (and doesn't shatter) because the amplitude of the waves (the actual physical displacement that creates the sound) is not sufficient to surpass the strength of the glass. To break the glass, you need to broadcast not only a sound that is 'just' the right frequency, but also has a high enough amplitude (loudness) to exceed the strength of the glass to resist those vibrations. In other words, if the force making the glass vibrate is big enough, the size of the vibration will become too large for the glass to resist. When the voice of the opera singer gets too loud for the glass to vibrate at its natural resonance, her voice shatters the glass.

Although I have been spending time exploring the science behind sound, it could be possible that God's intention to heal or bring deliverance or a change in our plight would be signified by a sound or vibrations that are only spiritually discerned. I am reminded of a verse of Scripture in Romans 8

Likewise the Spirit also helpeth our infirmities: for we know not what we should pray for as we ought: but the Spirit itself maketh intercession for us with groanings which cannot be uttered—Romans 8:26

Also, the Spirit helps us with our weakness. We do not know how to pray as we should. But the Spirit himself speaks to God for us, even begs God for us with deep feelings that words cannot explain
—Romans 8:26 (New Century Version)

So too the Holy Spirit comes to our aid and bears us up in our weakness; for we do not know what prayer to offer nor how to offer it worthily as we ought, but the Spirit Himself goes to meet our supplication and pleads in our behalf

with unspeakable yearnings and groanings too deep for utterance —Romans 8:26 (Amplified Version)

This is one of my favourite Scriptures and the other Bible versions I've quoted really help us to understand the work of the Holy Spirit in our times of affliction. In my times of difficulty and seasons of suffering, I have taken consolation from the fact that the Holy Spirit groans for me when I can't find the words.[35]

In this case the Greek word from which 'groanings is translated is *stenagmos* (sten-ag-mos') meaning a sigh. It is translated from another Greek word *stenazo* (sten-ad'-zo) which means to sigh, murmur, pray inaudibly. So, even though we can't hear it there are sounds being made on our behalf to God. I believe this Scripture is a great example and encouragement for us to know that the Holy Spirit prays, begs and pleads our case to God in our times of distress and trouble.

I Think I Hear A Sound...

Knowing that the Holy Spirit is at work 'making sounds' and our afflictions are also busy 'making sounds', I suppose we should be comforted and lift our faith to believe in our fast approaching deliverance and breakthrough. As faith is not about what we see but about what we believe, our prayer during these times should include a desire for the Lord to increase our faith.

I recall the tragic situation of the man who brought his son to Jesus. His son couldn't talk because he was possessed by a demon which caused his son to violently throw himself down on the ground, convulse, grind his teeth, foam at the mouth and become rigid. The father in his despair and with tears in his eyes cried out to Jesus, 'Lord, I believe; help thou mine unbelief.'[36]

I think this is a prayer we should pray when it feels like we are being overcome by our circumstances. This has become one of my prayers of desperation, over the years, "Jesus, I do believe! Help me to believe more!" I believe that as God increases our faith, the deafness of our panic mode subsides and we can then hear sounds, not physically but spiritually. And to those around us, we make absolutely no sense!

When we should be crumbling and falling and sinking into a dark and terrible place; we remain standing with a posture of belief and a perspective of hope. And then we can hear a sound... The sound of our deliverance approaching... The sound of our miracle... The sound of our breakthrough... The sound of victory... No one else can hear the sound because we are no longer focussed on the physical but the spiritual which makes us the epitome of walking scripture — **For we walk by faith, not by sight (2 Corinthians 5:7).** Our speech is then conducive to the spiritual place and not the physical place. It complements the liberating spiritual outlook and not a debilitating physical outlook — **We having the same spirit of faith, according as it is written, I believed, and therefore have I spoken; we also believe, and therefore speak (2 Corinthians 4:13).** So our speech changes when our perspective changes and what we speak about or decree or say is what comes into being. We know this because the Bible states that **'what we say can mean life or death' (Proverbs 18:21).**

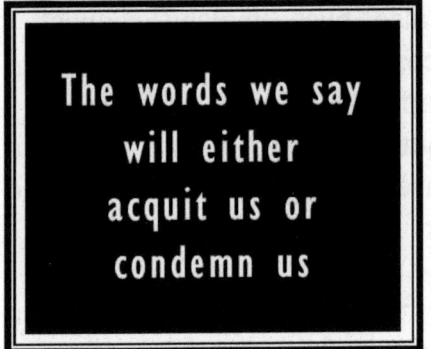

So we have to be careful what we say when we are going through our difficult and trying seasons because we can speak life to ourselves or death. Another way of putting it is to say that what comes out of our mouth can have a positive outcome or a negative one. This is confirmed by the words of Jesus in the New Testament who encouraged us not to speak hastily or without careful thought because **'the words we say will either acquit us or condemn us' (Matthew 12:37).**

It is clear that what we say has a profound effect on how things turn out. Or, let me put it this way, sound has an effect on the outcome of the predicaments we as believers can be facing at any given time. I believe speaking or decreeing as the Word of God and the Holy Spirit leads, makes us more receptive to what is happening in the spiritual realm. The more we read God's Word and allow ourselves to be led by the Holy Spirit, the more we will 'see' and 'hear'.

One particular Bible story about Elijah comes to mind. There had been no rain on the earth for three years[37] as the result of a Word from the Lord that Elijah had spoken to King Ahab because of the idol worship he had facilitated and permitted among God's people.[38] During this time of drought God had divinely arranged for Elijah to be cared for first by ravens and then by a widow.[39]

In the third year of the drought, Elijah challenges the prophets of Baal on Mount Carmel[40] to establish in the presence of the people, once and for all, who really is the almighty God. The result is a humiliating defeat for the prophets of Baal and a clear and unequivocal victory for Jehovah God, who demonstrates His supreme power in response to the prayer of Elijah, His prophet. The people, then seeing evidence of the God of Elijah make their choice as to which God they will serve.

It is after this showdown that Elijah tells Ahab to go and have a meal because he can **'hear the sound of the abundance of rain (1 Kings 18:41)'**. Elijah then goes to the top of Mount Carmel and stoops down to pray. He sends his servant to go and look towards the sea and report back what he sees. Now, Elijah told Ahab that he heard the sound of heavy rain but there is no sign that rain will fall, let alone heavy rainfall. However, Elijah knows what he has heard, I believe, by the Spirit so he sends his servant back to watch the horizon seven times.

On the seventh occasion the servant reports to Elijah that he can see a small cloud about the size of a man's hand coming up out of the sea. Elijah tells Ahab that he needs to get his chariot ready and go back down the mountain or he will be prevented from leaving by the rain that's on its way. And a little while later the sky became black with clouds and the winds blew and then the heavy rains came.

As we stay focused spiritually in our time of affliction and the Holy Spirit groans to God on our behalf and our affliction makes its own sound, there is a possibility that we, like Elijah, will hear a sound...

'Leannoth'—
Let's Sing Together

So we have established that every part of the body is vibrating. It follows then that each part of the body has its optimum, healthy frequency (rate of vibration). When we are ill, or sick or afflicted, it is because some part of us is not vibrating harmoniously with itself, the other parts, or its surroundings.

So then there is a possibility that this dissonance, or illness, may be rectified or healed with sound and intention, restoring the afflicted parts to their healthy frequency. When parts of the body do not work properly or vibrate out of harmony, it is called disease (dis-ease) — you are not at ease! Remember, one of the

> **When the body does not work or vibrate properly, it is called disease (dis-ease)**

meanings of 'Leannoth' is to sing together by course. So, by singing together or by making the right sound an atmosphere of ease or healing is released.

In my research I found an article in the Telegraph

Newspaper[41] about singing together. It stated that singing together (choral singing or practice) could be healthier than yoga! Also, that scientists have shown that not only does singing in a choir or singing together make you feel good, it has health benefits, too.

Researchers at the University of Gothenburg, Sweden, found that choristers' heartbeats synchronise when they sing together, bringing about a beneficial calming effect. The scientists asked a group of teenagers to perform 3 choral exercises – humming, singing a hymn and chanting – and then monitored their heart rhythms during each exercise. They were able to show that singing has a dramatic effect on heart rate variability, which is linked to a reduced risk of heart disease. The Gothenburg researchers also proved that with singing we can train our lungs to breathe better.

A similar study at Cardiff University in 2012 found that lung cancer patients who sang in a choir had a greater expiratory capacity than those who didn't. Singing has also been shown to boost our immune system, reduce stress levels and, according to a report published in the Journal of Music Therapy in 2004, help patients cope with chronic pain.

In a joint study by Harvard and Yale Universities in 2008 they went one step further, claiming that choral singing in a Connecticut town had increased residents' life expectancy.

Jeremy Hywel Williams, a leader of the Llanelli Choral Society in Wales said "Singing delivers a host of physical and emotional benefits, including increased aerobic exercise, improved breathing, improved posture, improved mind-set, improved confidence and improved self-esteem." He further pointed out that "While singing alone is good, singing with others can be even better."

Ok, so singing together is good... I suppose the next step would be to find out what the right sound is. As the ultimate source of our healing is Jehovah Raphah (pronounced raw-faw) — the God who heals us,[42] then we need to find out what sound the Father loves. Psalm 22:3 refers to God as the one who inhabits the praises of His people.

I am reminded of the time when the apostles Paul and Silas were put in prison in Macedonia.[43] They were beaten, put in a dungeon and their feet were placed in stocks. It would be normal to expect them to be very upset and spend their time complaining and discouraged but this is not what happened.

As midnight approached the apostles were heard praying and singing praises to God and suddenly there was a great earthquake; the prison foundations were shaken, all the doors flew open and all the prisoner's chains fell off! God divinely released them from their prison. Praise the Lord!

So as we sing and praise God in our times of affliction, we could say that we are providing the perfect atmosphere for

God to restore us to harmonious vibrations or for God's healing power to work. I know there are times when we pray, when we speak in tongues and when we lay hands but I would like to submit this perspective that sometimes our affliction experience requires us to sing like the apostles did to bring us to that place of healing. Actually, when you consider singing and music in general, it is important to note that music produces vibrations that affect the atmosphere and also our  bodies. Singing also produces vibrations that affect the atmosphere around us and also affect our bodies.

Other cultures and religions make use of singing in all kinds of ways. The Tibetan monks chant and use their singing bowls.[44] The Mongolians manipulate their pharynx or throat sing.[45] The Native Americans have been singing and chanting for years. Indigenous cultures use sound and produce sound that can affect the human body on all levels.

It seems to me that we who claim that we serve the true God who expects His people to give Him sincere worship and praise[46] are sometimes reluctant to believe that our praises touch God's heart and moves Him to respond to His people. While others are willing to explore the benefits of music and singing in times of affliction and suffering many of us scoff at the power and significance of music in the life of the believer. This is strange when you consider the fact that the construction and purpose of the Tabernacle of the Old Testament was designed using heaven as a template.[47]

God was quite specific when giving instructions to Moses for the building of the Tabernacle and also when he gave instructions to David for the building of the Temple. Apart from the directions pertaining to the sacrifices, structure and staffing provided by the Tribe of Levi, God also provided specific details on worship practices, singers and musical instruments.

After the construction of the Temple in Jerusalem by Solomon, David's son, it became the prominent focus of Jewish worship.[48] The emphasis of worship in the temple was primarily on sacrificial offerings and praise to God through music. The music was comprised of numerous and varied instruments of music, as well as well-trained vocal choirs (whose singing was perhaps somewhat similar to the melodious four-part harmony typical of the traditional church choir).

Numerous passages of Scripture refer to the music, both vocal and instrumental, used in worship to God during that time. 2 Samuel 6:5 says that, as the Ark of the Covenant was being brought to Jerusalem, David and all the house of Israel were celebrating before the Lord with all kinds of musical instruments.

In 1 Chronicles 15:16-24 David orders the Levite leaders to appoint a choir of Levites who were singers and musicians to sing joyful songs to the accompaniment of harps, lyres, and cymbals. They appointed Heman son of Joel along with others who were assistants and gatekeepers. Kenaniah, the head Levite, was chosen as the choir leader because of his skill. There were priests who were chosen to blow the trumpets as they marched in front of the Ark of God. We find this arrangement of singers and musicians confirmed in 1 Chronicles 16:4-6.

In 1 Chronicles 25:1 we also find that there was a prophetic element to their worship where the sons of Asaph and of Heman and of Jeduthun were set apart to prophesy with lyres, harps and cymbals. More details are outlined in 2 Chronicles 5:12-14 with an account of all the Levitical singers, Asaph, Heman, Jeduthun, and their sons and other relatives who were clothed in fine linen standing east of the altar with their musical instruments and one hundred and twenty priests blowing trumpets in unison. The trumpeters and the singers were to make themselves heard with one voice to praise and to glorify the Lord.

The Scripture states that when they lifted up their voice accompanied by trumpets, cymbals and the musical instruments the house of the Lord, was filled with the glory cloud of the Lord, so that the priests were unable to remain standing.

We also find an account in 2 Chronicles 29:25-30 of the worship practices instigated by Hezekiah in line with the command of King David, Gad the seer, and Nathan the prophet.

The worship accompanied the burnt offering on the altar. When the burnt offering began, the singers also began accompanied by the instruments of David and everyone worshipped. They also sang the words of David and Asaph the seer — the Psalms. There are numerous references to singing and the playing of instruments in worship to God throughout the Psalms: 33:1-3; 68:4, 25, 32; 81:1-3; 87:7; 92:1-3; 95:1-2; 98:1-8; 104:33; 105:2; 135:1-3; 137:1-6; 144:9; 149:1-6; 150:1-6. So, I think singing and music is very important in the life of the believer.

I suppose this is why when we come into services that focus on the healing power of God that the Praise and Worship is often extended and miracles often take place before the Word is preached or the laying on of hands. For me, it's simple — there is a link between our miracle and our worship and all that it entails.

We come to these services with disease (dis-ease) and sometimes we don't realise that the Lord has already started to deal with our affliction the moment we engage and participate in true and sincere Praise and Worship.

It makes sense that Paul encourages us to ensure that we do assemble ourselves together (Hebrews 10:25). So when we come together and pray together and praise together and worship together... we should remember that it's also important to... sing together...

Music Therapy—An Alternative Miracle?

Music Therapy is the use of music by health care professionals to promote healing and enhance the quality of life for their patients.[49] Music therapists work alongside other health care professionals such as doctors, nurses, speech therapists, psychologists and psychiatrists.

There is some evidence that, when used with conventional treatment, Music Therapy can help to reduce pain. For example, in cases with those suffering from cancer, it was found that one of the main reasons people with cancer used Music Therapy was because it made them feel good. Many of us know how calming and relaxing it can be to listen to a favourite piece of music. It can help people with cancer to cope with side effects such as pain, anxiety, depression and nausea.

Music Therapy can also be a safe place for people to explore fear, anxiety, anger and the range of emotional responses to living with cancer. Some studies show that Music Therapy can help children with cancer to cope, by encouraging them to cooperate and communicate.

Some studies have found that Music Therapy can lower rapid heart rate, reduce high blood pressure and breathing rate, and ease depression and sleeplessness. Music Therapy is often used in cancer treatment to help reduce the pain, anxiety, and nausea caused by chemotherapy. There are no claims that Music Therapy can cure cancer or other diseases, but medical experts do believe it can reduce some symptoms, aid healing, improve physical movement and enrich a patient's quality of life.

> **When you make music, it engages many different areas of the brain**

It has also been used to treat soldiers suffering from shell shock. Some scientific studies have shown the value of Music Therapy on the body, mind, and spirit of children and adults. However, it is apparent that the experience of listening to music widely varies in individuals.

This said, in recent years, scientists have made huge advances in understanding how the human brain processes music and how sound affects not just the mind but the body at large.

Here are seven things scientific research has discovered:[50]

1 Music can actually make you smarter!

It's no secret music has a serious impact on a person's

brain activity — whether that's how it engages different parts of the brain, how humans memorise tunes and lyrics or how different types of melodies and rhythms can elicit different emotional responses.

It's even been reported that ambient noise, played at a moderate volume, can encourage creativity, and that listening to music can help repair brain damage. The results are even better for musicians, particularly those who begin playing an instrument at an early age. According to some studies, music learning can encourage the development of stronger vocabularies and a better handle on nonverbal reasoning.

In the journal, News in Health, Harvard Medical School neuroscientist Gottfried Schlaug[51] even says that the nerve makeup of musicians differs from non-musicians, citing studies that musicians' minds have more bundles of nerves bridging the left side and right side of the brain. "When you make music, it engages many different areas of the brain, including visual, auditory and motor areas," Schlaug told News in Health. "That's why music making is also of potential interest in treating neurologic disorders."

2 Sad music doesn't necessarily make us sad
According to a study in Frontiers in Psychology in 2013,[52] sad music may not make you break down in tears. The findings suggest music can spark two types of emotional responses — perceived emotion and felt emotion. That means that though sad music is recognisably sad to many, experiencing it is not an emotionally darkening experience.

After conducting a survey of 44 participants, "the results revealed that the sad music was perceived to be more tragic, whereas the actual experiences of the participants listening to the sad music induced them to feel more romantic, blither, and less tragic emotions than they actually perceived with respect to the same music". "Thus, the participants experienced ambivalent emotions when they listened to the sad music."

3 Music is thought to have positive medicinal effects

Music has long been used in healing rituals around the world, and science suggests there's a good reason that's been the case.

In a 2006 thesis for Harvard University titled "The Effect of Music on the Human Body and Mind,"[53] written by Dawn Kent she refers to Plato who suggested using music to treat anxiety. She also mentioned Aristotle who categorised music as a therapeutic tool, particularly to treat those with volatile emotions. "Physiologically, music has a distinct effect on many biological processes,"

Kent wrote. "It inhibits the occurrence of fatigue, as well as changes the pulse and respiration rates, external blood pressure levels and psychogalvanic effect." (Both Plato and Aristotle are considered to be Fathers of Wester Philosophy)

As proof, Kent points to Michelle Lefevre's 2004 book, Playing With Sound: The Therapeutic Use of Music in Direct Work With Children,[54] which argues that high-pitched tones can sometimes lead to feelings of panic and increased anxiety. One theory even introduces something called the "Mozart Effect,"[55] and a study that builds on the theory found that the infamous composer's "Piano Sonata in D Major" led to decreased epilepsy in patients — a finding that even extended to patients in comas.

4 Mood music is a thing

"Music can increase one's libido," said Curtis Levang [56] a clinical psychologist and marriage and family therapist, Everyday Health reported. And speaking to the publication, urologist Y. Mark Hong said music and sex are alike, in that both can be emotionally charged experiences. Therefore, he said, it's possible music can help men with low testosterone to up their sex drives, as listening to music can elevate serotonin levels in a person's body. And it's even possible that music can help singles secure a date.

> Listening to music can elevate serotonin levels in a person's body

According to a study by researchers in France, single women who had listened to romantic music were more likely to hand out their phone numbers than those participants who had listened to neutral music prior to being asked out. Although, I should stress that I am only citing this article for the science and in no way am I suggesting that single women go and listen to some romantic music and start handing out their personal details to all and sundry!

5 Music can help you go the distance

Several studies have shown that music can boost endurance and help us use energy more efficiently during exercise. One 2012 study called "Effect of Music-Movement Synchrony on Exercise Oxygen Consumption" found cyclists who peddled along to music used 7% less oxygen than those who didn't couple their ride with music to match their pace.

According to the study, which was published in the Scientific American, a song's beats per minute (bpm) has an effect on motivation — though that's true only up to a certain threshold. "The most recent research suggests that a ceiling effect occurs around 145 bpm: Anything higher does not seem to contribute much additional motivation," the Scientific American wrote, "On occasion, the speed and flow of the lyrics supersede the underlying beat: Some people work out to rap songs, for example, with dense, swiftly spoken lyrics overlaid on a relatively mellow melody."

For reference, Bruce Springsteen's "Born to Run," Spoon's "Don't Make Me a Target" and the Beach Boys' "Do You Wanna Dance" all clock in at 147 bpm. Spotify has come to similar conclusions, and in 2015 debuted Spotify Running[57] in response to those findings, adding tech to its platform that tracks a runner's pace and curating a playlist of songs that match that pace.

6 Music can help you adjust that attitude

According to research conducted at the University of Missouri, a team of scientists have confirmed what has perhaps been long suspected: Music is a mood booster. Healthline reports that the study's lead author, Yuna Ferguson, said in a press release, "Our work provides support for what many people already do — listen to music to improve their moods,"

7 Singing in the shower may actually be good for you.

Writing for Jweekly, Dr. Jerry Saliman,[58] who is retired from the Kaiser Permanente South San Francisco Medical Centre, argued there are health benefits to singing out loud — particularly for the elderly. "Studies have shown that singing can improve the brain functionality of seniors suffering from conditions such as aphasia and Parkinson's disease," Saliman writes. "In addition, many seniors live alone, are limited in mobility due to chronic conditions such as arthritis and are on budgets; finding easy and affordable activities that keep them engaged and connected is beneficial for their emotional well-being."

> Studies have shown that singing can improve brain functionality

Saliman also wrote that singing has also been found to improve the respiration health and functionality of patients with chronic obstructive pulmonary disease, and those patients with chronic obstructive pulmonary disease who sing report less feelings of breathlessness. So, in short, music has the ability of altering one's experience and releasing a selection of different sensations, as well as a feeling of release and solace.

I also found out that verbal IQ is improved – the verbal and visual skills are improved especially when an individual practices on the piano. This was found in the study of individuals aged between 8 and 11 years who were able to develop a higher level of IQ verbally when they took extra-curricular music classes. This showed that the practice of the musical instrument developed visual and cognitive perception. Also, for many, happiness is increased when listening to music according to results from a study carried out in 2013 by Sheldon and Ferguson.[59]

Listening and participating in music is also beneficial to those suffering from heart disease. Anxiety and stress is one of the main causes of heart disease and a study showed that when music was enjoyed by over 1500 patients, it reduced the blood pressure and heart rate that lead to anxiety and heart disease.

There is also a correlation between music and restoring vision. When an individual has a stroke it is often the case that the part of the brain that deals with vision is damaged. The patient may then not be aware of certain objects and may have trouble seeing them. Studies have shown however, that when these patients listen to their favourite music, the vision was improved and in many cases restored.

So then, we understand that it can be said that illness is a manifestation of dis-harmony or dis-ease within the body — an imbalance in the cells or a given organ. Since all matter is energy vibrating at different rates, by altering the rate of vibration we can change the structure of matter or change the atmosphere. What does singing do? What does music do? It alters vibrations! It changes the atmosphere!

Well, if the scientists are happy to connect recovery, improved prognosis and for want of another word, healing to sound... to music... to singing, what say we? Perhaps it is no coincidence that God gives the barren clear instructions in His Word:

Sing, O barren, thou that didst not bear; break forth into singing, and cry aloud, thou that didst not travail with child: for more are the children of the desolate than the children of the married wife, saith the Lord —Isaiah 54:1

The Lord says, "Sing, Jerusalem. You are like a woman who never gave birth to children. Start singing and shout for joy. You never felt the pain of giving birth, but you will have more children than the woman who has a husband. — Isaiah 54:1 (New Century Version)

The barren, childless one is told to sing loudly and joyously in anticipation of a promised and wonderful change in their circumstances.

God also tells His people who have been enslaved in foreign countries to sing and be happy because He will bring them back to Jerusalem and restore their lands:

Thus saith the Lord; Sing with gladness for Jacob, and shout among the chief of the nations: publish ye, praise ye, and say, O Lord, save thy people, the remnant of Israel. Behold, I will bring them from the north country, and gather them from the coasts of the earth, and with them the blind and the lame, the woman with child and her that travaileth with child together: a great company shall return thither —Jeremiah 31:7-8

In fact, God doesn't just say, sing — He says to sing with gladness. God expects us, in our time of suffering to sing joyfully and happily! Wow! But it's not impossible. I've realised that often when attending our church services, we may enter the building not feeling so good or particularly elated or upbeat but when the Praise and Worship begins, the music and singing begin to have an effect. Before we realise it, we feel good and happy and I believe this is the perfect and optimum atmosphere for the healing and the miraculous power of God to do His work. So sing!

It seems to me that singing is not just singing. It's not just making beautiful melodies or harmonious sounds. There is more going on. In fact I don't think it even matters if you're tone deaf or sing off key!

Your 'singing abilities' may not be sweet music to the human ear but it definitely has a positive effect on God's ear, so sing! And it seems that in our difficult times and in the pain of our affliction, we are told to sing *before* we have received our breakthrough. We are expected to rejoice *before* the time of our relief. To posture ourselves in praise to our God *before* He turns our sadness to joy.

So, if this is a difficult time for you or perhaps this is a chapter in your life where you are struggling with illness or some other debilitating situation or if you see this as your season of affliction, SING. I'm not saying to stop taking the medication or other conventional remedies, or to stop praying or fasting but along with all of what you may be doing, remember to sing.

In scripture, there are many accounts of Jehovah God who responds when His people pray and when His people make sacrifices but I also found an account in the Bible where He responds when His people sing.

And when they began to sing and to praise, the Lord set ambushments against the children of Ammon, Moab, and mount Seir, which were come against   Judah;   and they were   smitten —2 Chronicles 20:22

At the very moment they began to sing and give praise, the Lord caused the armies of Ammon, Moab, and Mount Seir

to start fighting among themselves —2 Chronicles 20:22 (New Living Translation)

I think by now we should realise how awesome singing is and how amazing it is that our God responds not only when we pray but also when we sing.

The psalmist David when he composed Psalm 32, referred to the hiding place of God and spoke about how the Lord compassed or surrounded him with songs of deliverance (Psalm 32:7). In a time of reflection he appreciated the place of peace and sweet comfort that those songs and music strains provided.

Singing must have been of some importance because Solomon wrote 1005 songs! (1 Kings 4:32). The Bible mentions various songs inspired by different events or situations or composed as memorials to the wondrous acts and works of Jehovah.

Some are self-explanatory — Song of Loves,[60] Song of Fools,[61] Song of Songs,[62] Song of the Lamb,[63] Song of the Lord,[64] Song of Degrees,[65] Song of Moses,[66] Song of Asaph.[67] However, I think that the songs that God's people most appreciated would have been those Songs of Deliverance. I don't know what their melody sounded like or the timing of the music but whatever the details of these songs were, they enveloped the psalmist in just what they needed during their time of trial.

To me, the Songs of Deliverance can be likened to some of the old hymns my mum taught me as a child. I can still remember the words and beautiful melodies. She would hum to herself while she cooked or sing them while she sat at her sewing machine. She loved their three and four part harmonies and she would teach them to my sister and me. Mum wouldn't let us stop practicing until it was perfect. Sometimes we would be singing for hours while thinking there could be much more fun things we could be doing at the time.

Now, when I look back I appreciate every single moment we spent practicing those old hymns. They have been a source of encouragement and strength to me over the years. They have indeed been my very own Songs of Deliverance. Every now and then a chorus or a refrain comes to mind. The words of the verses always perfectly suit the moment and the melodies are always uplifting. These are some of my favourites — I wish you could hear the melodies but hopefully the words will give you some idea of how deeply soul-touching these old hymns are!

Sweet hour of prayer! Sweet hour of prayer![68]
That calls me from a world of care,
And bids me at my Father's throne
Make all my wants and wishes known.
In seasons of distress and grief,
My soul has often found relief,
And oft escaped the tempter's snare
By thy return, sweet hour of prayer!

Sweet hour of prayer! Sweet hour of prayer!
The joys I feel, the bliss I share
Of those whose anxious spirits burn
With strong desires for thy return!
With such I hasten to the place
Where God my Saviour shows his face,
And gladly take my station there,
And wait for thee, sweet hour of prayer!

Sweet hour of prayer! Sweet hour of prayer!
Thy wings shall my petition bear
To him whose truth and faithfulness
Engage the waiting soul to bless.
And since he bids me seek his face,
Believe his word, and trust his grace,
I'll cast on him my every care,
And wait for thee, sweet hour of prayer!

My Jesus, I love thee, I know thou art mine;[69]
For thee all the follies of sin I resign;
My gracious Redeemer, my Saviour art thou;
If ever I loved thee, my Jesus, 'tis now.

I love thee because thou hast first loved me
And purchased my pardon on Calvary's tree;
I love thee for wearing the thorns on thy brow;
If ever I loved thee, my Jesus, 'tis now.

I'll love thee in life, I will love thee in death,
And praise thee as long as thou lendest me breath,

And say when the death dew lies cold on my brow:
If ever I loved thee, my Jesus, 'tis now.

In mansions of glory and endless delight,
I'll ever adore thee in heaven so bright;
I'll sing with the glittering crown on my brow:
If ever I loved thee, my Jesus, 'tis now.

There is a land of pure delight,[70]
Where saints immortal reign;
Infinite day excludes the night,
And pleasures banish pain.
There everlasting spring abides,
And never-withering flowers;
Death, like a narrow sea, divides
That heavenly land from ours.

Sweet fields beyond the swelling flood
Stand dressed in living green;
So to the Jews old Canaan stood,
While Jordan rolled between.
But timorous mortals start and shrink
To cross the narrow sea,
And linger shivering on the brink,
And fear to launch away.

O could we make our doubts remove,
Those gloomy doubts that rise,
And see the Canaan that we love
With unbeclouded eyes;

Could we but climb where Moses stood,
And view the landscape o'er,
Not Jordan's stream, nor death's cold flood,
Should fright us from the shore!

I need thee every hour,[71]
Most gracious Lord;
No tender voice like thine
Can peace afford.

I need thee, O I need thee,
every hour I need thee.
O bless me now, my Savior;
I come to thee.

I need thee every hour;
Stay thou near by;
Temptations lose their power
When thou art nigh.

I need thee every hour,
In joy or pain;
Come quickly and abide,
Or life is vain.

I need thee every hour;
Teach me thy will;
And thy rich promises
In me fulfil.

I need thee every hour,
Most Holy One;
O make me thine indeed,
Thou Blessed Son!

Guide me, O my great Redeemer,[72]
Pilgrim through this barren land;
I am weak, but you are mighty;
Hold me with your powerful hand.

Bread of heaven, bread of heaven,
Feed me now and evermore,
Feed me now and evermore.

Open now the crystal fountain,
Where the healing waters flow.
Let the fire and cloudy pillar
Lead me all my journey through.

Strong Deliverer, strong Deliverer,
Ever be my strength and shield,
Ever be my strength and shield.

When I tread the verge of Jordan,
Bid my anxious fears subside.
Death of death, and hell's Destruction,
Land me safe on Canaan's side.

Songs of praises, songs of praises
I will ever sing to you,
I will ever sing to you.

Father, I stretch my hands to thee,[73]
No other help I know;
If Thou withdraw Thyself from me,
Ah! Whither shall I go?

On Thy dear Son I now believe
O let me feel Thy power
And all my varied wants relieve
In this accepted hour

Author of faith! to Thee I lift
My weary longing eyes
O let me now receive this gift
My soul without it dies

Surely Thou canst not let me die;
O speak, and I shall live;
And here I will unwearied lie,
Till Thou Thy Spirit give.

How would my fainting soul rejoice
Could I but see Thy face
Now let me hear Thy quickening voice
And taste Thy pardoning grace

I do believe, I now believe
That Jesus died for me.
And that He shed His precious blood
From sin to set me free

I could go on and on because I just really love those old hymns and hopefully you can see how deeply moving these hymns are. Whether you love singing the old hymns like me or are drawn to the more modern praise and worship songs and choruses, the main point is that no matter what your circumstances are you should always remember to sing praises to God. In fact the psalmist encourages God's people to come into His presence singing (Psalm 100:2).

Miguel de Cervantes[74] was a Spanish writer who is highly regarded as perhaps the greatest writer in the Spanish language and one of the world's pre-eminent novelists. I love the words that he said during a period of illness, "He who sings frightens away his ills."

I stated this before and I reiterate — The Mongolians manipulate their pharynx, the Tibetans and the Native Americans chant so I choose to sing to my God, Jehovah Raphah – My healer, King of Kings and Lord of Lords, who has the power to do mighty miracles. Indeed, I choose to sing to Him!

Affliction Is Good!

It is good for me that I have been afflicted; that I might learn thy statutes —Psalm 119:71

Even though for the most part I have focused on ways in which music and singing and sound help to alleviate our plight of affliction, I wouldn't do this subject justice if I didn't mention one other point — in some cases affliction is good! This is often hard for one to accept but it is a Biblical principle so for us as believers we

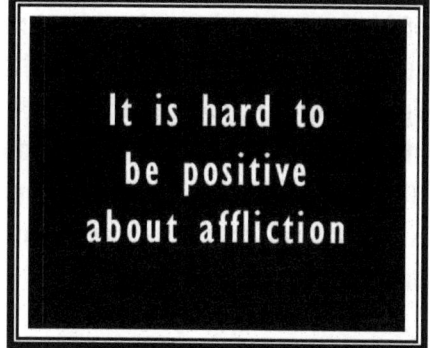

should be willing to explore this particularly difficult area of affliction.

The psalmist, in Psalm 119, came to the conclusion that affliction is good. Somehow he was able to see that it was a good thing for him to be afflicted and that it was a good thing for him to suffer. The reason he cited was that during his time of affliction he was learning the statutes of God. That somehow his season of suffering taught him how to pay attention to God's laws and that affliction came with valuable lessons.

So it would seem that affliction has a purpose. This could mean that we can remain in a season of affliction until that season has served its purpose. That God will not allow that season of suffering to end — He will not bring us out until we have learnt those valuable lessons. However, we can be assured that once God's purpose has been served, He will bring you out.

Go, and gather the elders of Israel together, and say unto them, The Lord God of your fathers, the God of Abraham, of Isaac, and of Jacob, appeared unto me, saying, I have surely visited you, and seen that which is done to you in Egypt: And I have said, I will bring you up out of the affliction of Egypt unto the land of the Canaanites, and the Hittites, and the Amorites, and the Perizzites, and the Hivites, and the Jebusites, unto a land flowing with milk and honey—Exodus 3:16-22

He proved Himself time and time again to His people that He was a God who delivers his people from their affliction. In this passage of Scripture, the word affliction in the Hebrew means 'distress or suffering and the cause of this.' It means 'depression, i.e. misery, trouble; depressed, in mind or circumstances.' The Webster's Dictionary defines 'affliction' as 'the state of being afflicted; the cause of persistent pain or distress; great suffering; the state of being affected by something that causes pain or unhappiness.'

When you read these definitions it is hard to be positive about affliction but in spite of this it is important to realise that there's a purpose to our affliction. I have found out that there is a consensus among several schools of thought that for us as believers affliction or suffering brings about the purifying of the believer as he or she identifies with Christ.

The Apostle Paul, in his letter to the church at Thessalonica commended them as examples to the churches at Macedonia and Greece. In spite of their trials and suffering they accepted the gospel with joy.

Knowing, brethren beloved, your election of God. For our gospel came not unto you in word only, but also in power, and in the Holy Ghost, and in much assurance; as ye know what manner of men we were among you for your sake. And ye became followers of us, and of the Lord, having received the word in much affliction, with joy of the Holy Ghost: So that ye were ensamples to all that believe in Macedonia and Achaia—1 Thessalonians 1:4-7

In his letter to the Romans the Apostle Paul also pointed out his standpoint that we should rejoice when we run into problems and trials, for we know that they are good for us — they help us learn to be patient and endure which then develops strength of character in us showing a reason and a purpose for our times of adversity.

And not only so, but we glory in tribulations also: knowing that tribulation worketh patience; And patience,

experience; and experience, hope: And hope maketh not ashamed; because the love of God is shed abroad in our hearts by the Holy Ghost which is given unto us —Romans 5:3-5

So, we begin to see that there is a purpose to our affliction and the psalmist was able to see it in spite of his pain. We could possibly begin to see things from the psalmists' perspective. The psalmist then postures himself to commend God on his affliction experiences in that his suffering had made him more receptive to God's Word, His laws and His ways.

Blessed is the man whom thou chastenest, O Lord, and teachest him out of thy law —Psalm 94:12

Before I was afflicted I went astray: but now have I kept thy word. —Psalm 119:67

The purification function of the trials we experience is illustrated in certain passages where the metaphor used is the process of refining metals in fire and smelting out the dross[75] the impure unwanted material that forms on the surface of molten metal.

And I will turn my hand upon thee, and purely purge away thy dross, and take away all thy tin —Isaiah 1:25

I will raise my fist against you. I will melt you down and skim off your slag. I will remove all your impurities —Isaiah 1:25 New Living Translation

And I will bring the third part through the fire, and will refine them as silver is refined, and will try them as gold is tried: they shall call on my name, and I will hear them: I will say, It is my people: and they shall say, The Lord is my God
—Zechariah 13:9

The third that is left I will test with fire, purifying them like silver, testing them like gold. Then they will call on me, and I will answer them. I will say, 'You are my people,' and they will say, 'The Lord is our God
—Zechariah 13:9 New Century version

But who may abide the day of his coming? and who shall stand when he appeareth? for he is like a refiner's fire, and like fullers' soap —Malachi 3:2

But who can live when he appears? Who can endure his coming? For he is like a blazing fire refining precious metal, and he can bleach the dirtiest garments —Malachi 3:2 (The Living Bible)

If we apply the analogy portrayed in these verses we can ascertain that God's purpose during our times of affliction is to remove any impurities or sin from our lives. This is further testified to when we look at the story of Job in the Bible and all that he suffered. Although, he went through times of despair and feeling like God had abandoned him, there was a time where he seems to see clearly all that God has purposed through His suffering. Job comes to a remarkable conclusion seeing the purpose of His suffering as good.

Behold, I go forward, but he is not there; and backward, but I cannot perceive him: On the left hand, where he doth work, but I cannot behold him: he hideth himself on the right hand, that I cannot see him: But he knoweth the way that I take: when he hath tried me, I shall come forth as gold —Job 23:8-10

But I search in vain. I seek him here, I seek him there and cannot find him. I seek him in his workshop in the North but cannot find him there; nor can I find him in the South; there, too, he hides himself. But he knows every detail of what is happening to me; and when he has examined me, he will pronounce me completely innocent — as pure as solid gold —Job 23:8-10 (The Living Bible)

I always feel encouraged when I read these verses. They help me to re-focus and continue to trust that God has a perfect plan that He is working out through my suffering.

We can also gain strength and hope that God's plan and purpose is being worked out during these difficult seasons when we look at the sufferings of Jesus. Isaiah prophetically documents Christ's suffering, painting a vivid picture which we see come to life in the pages of the New Testament.

Behold, my servant shall deal prudently, he shall be exalted and extolled, and be very high. As many were astonied at thee; his visage was so marred more than any man, and his form more than the sons of men
—Isaiah 52:13-14

See, my Servant shall prosper; he shall be highly exalted. Yet many shall be amazed when they see him-yes, even far-off foreign nations and their kings; they shall stand dumbfounded, speechless in his presence. For they shall see and understand what they had not been told before. They shall see my Servant beaten and bloodied, so disfigured one would scarcely know it was a person standing there —Isaiah 52:13-14 (The Living Bible)

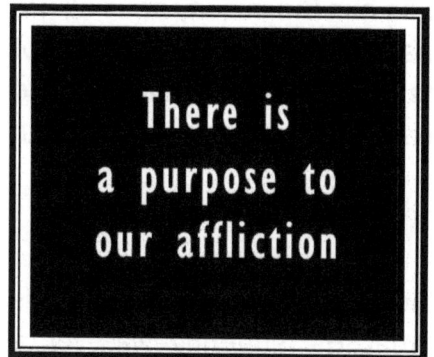

There is
a purpose to
our affliction

Isaiah speaks about the high honour that will be given to Jesus but he also mentions how awful his suffering will be. On the face of it, it would seem as if there could be no justification to what Jesus suffered but I've come to learn that God always has a divine reason. I may not know what it is but I trust Him to work His purpose out in my life.

Yes, there is a purpose to our affliction in that the experiences that we go through purify us in the same way the refinery purifies metals at high temperatures. Jesus provides a perfect example for us as we look at how He coped in His times of suffering. We can learn from Jesus how to posture ourselves appropriately in our seasons of affliction. Isaiah goes on to describe in more detail what Jesus suffered and how he reacted to his suffering.

He is despised and rejected of men; a man of sorrows, and acquainted with grief: and we hid as it were our faces from him; he was despised, and we esteemed him not. Surely he hath borne our griefs, and carried our sorrows: yet we did esteem him stricken, smitten of God, and afflicted. But he was wounded for our transgressions, he was bruised for our iniquities: the chastisement of our peace was upon him; and with his stripes we are healed. All we like sheep have gone astray; we have turned every one to his own way; and the Lord hath laid on him the iniquity of us all. He was oppressed, and he was afflicted, yet he opened not his mouth: he is brought as a lamb to the slaughter, and as a sheep before her shearers is dumb, so he openeth not his mouth.
—Isaiah 53:3-7

Jesus understood that there was a purpose to His affliction. He understood that His suffering was for a reason — to redeem the souls of mankind.

Some of the stuff we are experiencing makes us, like Christ, unrecognisable and in some cases unpresentable and intolerable. We can be difficult to be around and/or we purposely retreat from life and from people. It's hard to stay positive when you're in pain or when nothing ever seems to work out or go well.

I've learnt that keeping in mind that God really is purposing something divine and marvellous is helpful. I can be more positive about my circumstances rather than only focusing on the negative, my pain and bad feelings.

I have also found out when looking further into this subject of affliction that during our time of affliction, every now and then, God does some amazing things! When I looked at some of the characters in the Bible who went through affliction, I must admit that I felt encouraged and definitely filled with hope. Jacob worked for his uncle, Laban who didn't treat him fairly but God intervened.

Except the God of my father, the God of Abraham, and the fear of Isaac, had been with me, surely thou hadst sent me away now empty. God hath seen mine affliction and the labour of my hands, and rebuked thee yesternight —Genesis 31:42

But the God of my father, the God of Abraham and the God of Isaac, was with me. Otherwise, you would have sent me away with nothing. But he saw the trouble I had and the hard work I did, and last night he corrected you —Genesis 31:42 New Century Version

Even while suffering God will bless you in some special way and bring some relief to your plight. Joseph, after all he had suffered was able to testify to this fact. In the place where God tested him, God also blessed him.

And Joseph called the name of the firstborn Manasseh: For God, said he, hath made me forget all my toil, and all my father's house. And the name of the second called he Ephraim: For God hath caused me to be fruitful in the land of my affliction —Genesis 41:51-52

Isn't it just like God to show you how blessed you are even in your times of suffering? And when we begin to have this more positive outlook, we may not realise it but His purification process is in full force!

If we, as believers are able to positively posture ourselves and willingly align ourselves with the Lord as He works on us, then we will also be able to help others who are struggling in this area.

It does feel more natural to turn yourself inward, so to speak, and hide away while you hope for your change in circumstances but what God really wants us to do is reach out to others. We see this happening with the believers of the New Testament Church who were facing all kinds of suffering, afflictions and persecutions. In spite of all that they were going through they still managed to help each other and encourage one another.

The Apostle Paul wrote to the Corinthian church about what was happening with the churches in Macedonia. How, in spite of the fact that they were going through much trouble, hard times and extreme poverty, they helped one another by giving to one another, not what they could afford but much more (2 Corinthians 8:1-3).

And when writing to the church in Thessalonica he commented on how moved and encouraged he was by their faith and generosity and how the fact that they were standing true to God helped him to bear up during his crushing troubles and suffering. Paul actually stated that he could bear anything as long as he knew that they were remaining strong in Christ (1 Thessalonians 3:6-8).

I have mentioned the Apostle Paul in a previous chapter but just want to reiterate his own perspective on affliction and its merits. He encourages the believer by making a comparison — highlighting the fact that our present suffering cannot be compared to God's glory that will shine and emanate from us at the conclusion of His process.

For I reckon that the sufferings of this present time are not worthy to be compared with the glory which shall be revealed in us —Romans 8:18

(But what of that?) For I consider that the sufferings of this present time (this present life) are not worth being compared with the glory that is about to be revealed to us and in us and for us and conferred on us!
—Romans 8:18 (The Amplified Bible)

He reaffirms this standpoint in the second epistle to the Corinthians stressing the point that our season of affliction is working for us and not as we sometimes feel, against us.

The apostle Paul calls what we are going through 'light'

affliction! I don't know if I would describe it that way but I have to agree with him that the work that our affliction seasons are doing will result in God's glorious power manifested in our lives.

For our light affliction, which is but for a moment, worketh for us a far more exceeding and eternal weight of glory
—2 Corinthians 4:17

These troubles and sufferings of ours are, after all, quite small and won't last very long. Yet this short time of distress will result in God's richest blessing upon us forever and ever!
—2 Corinthians 4:17 (The Living Bible)

So, like the Apostle Paul, I focus on the future and pray that the Lord helps me to see or learn or know or understand or be receptive to all that He is doing in my seasons of affliction.

I may not understand everything and truth be told, nothing may make any sense to me because who can really understand the mind of God? (Isaiah 55:8-9). His thoughts far surpass ours and His ways are truly difficult to work out. Often nothing seems to make sense and we can find ourselves wondering if our heavenly Father has lost the plot when it comes to stuff concerning us. I could go on but I won't! I think you can see where I'm coming from...

All of this said, this is where I end up — I have decided that while my affliction makes its own sound, whatever I don't understand, I pray that the Holy Spirit gives me His peace concerning it so that I can walk through, and crawl through, and pray through, and praise through, and worship through, and sigh through and of course... sing through!... every moment by His grace.

Sing Anyway...!

As I bring my deliberations to a close in this final chapter I take the opportunity to collate my thoughts and prepare myself to adjust my posture and attitude to my seasons of affliction. And hopefully, while my affliction cries out to God, I will be able to sing!

When the disciples asked Jesus about what would happen at the end of the world and what signs would help them recognise when He would return. He listed what the end times would be like but He also made reference to the type of affliction people would be going through.

For in those days shall be affliction, such as was not from the beginning of the creation which God created unto this time, neither shall be —Mark 13:19

Those days will be full of trouble. There will be more trouble than there has ever been since the beginning, when God made the world, until now, and nothing as bad will ever happen again —Mark 13:19 New Century Version

As I was studying affliction, I came across this verse and realised that in the end times as the time of the return of Jesus Christ approaches, affliction will become a familiar experience for the believer. In fact, Jesus said that there is a time coming when God's people will experience affliction like never before and that He will shorten the time of that calamity to ensure His people are able to survive such a terrible ordeal (Mark 13:20).

The Greek word which is interpreted affliction[76] in this verse means 'terrible affliction and terrible trouble; pressure; persecution and tribulation.' It would be wonderful to think that we could say goodbye to affliction forever but that will not be the case until Christ returns. So, until then God has provided ways for us to cope and live through our seasons of affliction until our time of release. Sometimes you may pray. Sometimes you may fast and pray. Sometimes you may read and meditate on the Word. Sometimes you may praise and worship. And sometimes you may receive encouragement from other believers as we know iron sharpens iron (Proverbs 27:17). Whatever you feel led or inspired to do in those dark moments, I hope that every now and then you will be inspired to sing.

> **When we sing— It's the right side of the brain that we rely upon**

Remember, it has been scientifically proven that we are better off when we sing. Although singing and speech both involve the larynx[77] and the vocal cords modulating or manipulating the air as it is pushed out of the lungs, they stem from different sides of the brain. When we speak, the left-hand side is involved — the part that controls word formation and sentence structure. But when we sing, it is the right hemisphere of the brain that we rely upon, to produce the rhythm and melody of music.[78] Someone might have a speech impediment but it won't be apparent when they sing — because it's a different part of the brain. So stutterers learn to speak fluently by learning to sing their sentences and stroke victims learn to talk again using music. When you sing, even heavy regional accents are less noticeable.

The other point to note is that happiness depends a lot on which side of the brain we use.[79] When you feel under pressure, your brain is telling you that you have been using the left hemisphere of your brain to its maximum capacity. 85% of the time, we function using the left hemisphere of our brain.

We make sense of things, think of sequences, analyse language and meaning, interpret information and communication and absorb new facts from all around us. Although these functions are necessary to our life, the left side of our brain has its limits and uses pressure to signal that we need to let go and switch to using the right side of our brain.

The best way to change the balance and turn off the warning signs is to use the right brain more. Fun things we enjoy and love doing can do this straight way. Laughing, dancing, listening to music, singing, doing art and playing with animals can make a huge shift in our level of pressure.

The right hemisphere of the brain is also activated when you hear melodies with a variety of pitch and timbre. Music results in a heightened spiritual experience. The use of the right brain releases endorphins, making us feel good. Endorphins are "feel good" chemicals that trigger fun, enjoyment, happiness and relaxation. These chemicals also fight illness very well, help us boost our immune system and handle pain better.

So whether we look at it from a scientific point of view or a spiritual point of view, singing is good for us especially when we feel pressured or afflicted. The Hungarian composer, Zoltan Kodaly[80] said that 'Music is the manifestation of the human spirit'.

It's wonderful to know and understand the science behind singing but I have to also agree with Kodaly that there is definitely a spiritual aspect to singing. So on that 'note' — pun intended! I would like to remind you to keep singing whatever your situation, just

> **200 singers returned home to Jerusalem and Judah from Babylon**

like God's people have done throughout the centuries. They sang before they could see a solution. They sang while they struggled through adversity. They sang after receiving victory. God's people have always been singing people and we as believers should be no different. Sing like Moses and Miriam who celebrated their deliverance from Pharaoh and his armies who God drowned in the Red Sea (Exodus 15:1, 21). Sing like Deborah who praised God for giving the Israelites victory over Jabin the king of Canaan (Judges 5:1-3). Sing like David who thanked God for delivering him from his enemies (2 Samuel 22:1) and who praised God when he brought the Ark of the Lord back to its place (1 Chronicles 16:7-9). Sing like the Israelite women who celebrated David's victory over the Philistine giant, Goliath (1 Samuel 18:6-7).

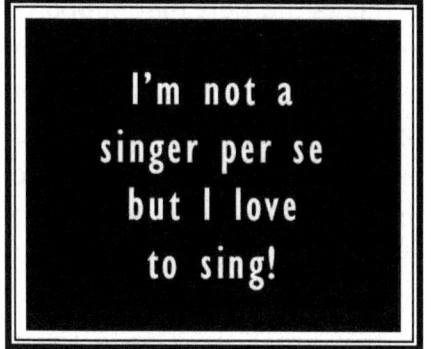

I'm not a singer per se but I love to sing!

Sometimes we will sing like the Israelite mourners who lamented the death of Josiah King of Judah. Sing like those who returned home to Jerusalem and Judah from captivity in Babylon, which included 200 singers (Ezra 2:1, 65). Sing like the Israelites who praised God at the dedication of the wall of Jerusalem (Nehemiah 12:27). Sing like Zion who praised God who had removed their enemies from their city and promised that they would no longer see evil any more (Zephaniah 3:14-15). I could go on and on and on but I think you get my drift.

As I continue to ponder I am reminded of references to the significance of singing mentioned in the New Testament. In Paul's letter to the Ephesians he encouraged them, noting that they were living in difficult times and that they should be careful how they behave. He stressed that they should not act foolishly but to be wise and grasp every opportunity they have to do good. Paul also pointed out the importance of not acting rashly or thoughtlessly, but to carefully try to find out and do whatever the Lord would want them to and live in the way that Lord would expect them to.

He mentioned that they should be careful not to drink too much wine, because it will only lead to trouble. Instead, he said they should be filled with the Holy Spirit and controlled by Him. Then, and this is the part that supports our journey to this point, he encouraged the believers of Ephesus to always give thanks to Jehovah God for everything, talk about Jesus a lot quoting Psalms and hymns, singing sacred songs and making their own music in their hearts focused on the Lord (Ephesians 5:15-20).

Paul pointed out that it would help the believers if they committed themselves to certain practices. One area of practice that Paul relayed was that of making their own music, meditating on the Psalms and singing spiritual songs. Paul also conveyed a similar instruction to the Colossians:

Let the word of Christ dwell in you richly in all wisdom; teaching and admonishing one another in psalms and hymns and spiritual songs, singing with grace in your hearts to the Lord —Colossians 3:16

For me, it is clear that our Christian life should involve the regular practice of singing and we should believe that we will receive all the practical, physical and spiritual benefits that result from its participation.

There is also a deeper spiritual perspective that Paul mentions when writing to the Christians in Corinth. When, clarifying how best to edify the church when the spiritual gift of unknown tongues was present, he pointed out that he did not only speak in tongues but also sang in tongues, or as the King James Version puts it, he would 'sing with the Spirit' (1 Corinthians 14:15).

I have found when I am in prolonged and deep worship to God that I flow with ease in singing in the Spirit or singing in tongues. It's at those moments I feel the most closest to God and those around me are acutely aware of the tangible presence of God's Holy Spirit doing His work. All I can say is that it's a mystery.

I am reminded of a verse in the New Testament that refers to this fact — that when we speak in an unknown tongue we speak to God not men and that no person can understand because in the Spirit we speak mysteries or secret and hidden things (1 Corinthians 14:2). I may not know exactly what God is doing when I sing but I do know that He is doing something!

The last scripture I would like to make reference to is James 5:13 - **Is any among you afflicted? Let him pray. Is any merry? Let him sing psalms.** As I read this verse I looked at the Greek meaning for the word 'pray' and found that it has several meanings. It does mean 'to pray to

God' but it also means 'to supplicate, to worship.'[81] I believe we can come to the conclusion that as we pray to God, it shouldn't only be a time of requests but also a time of worship – a time of praise and without doubt, a time of singing.

I'm not a singer per se but I do love to sing! I am definitely not a remarkable singer so I don't have the vocal range of Whitney Houston or the mellow tones of CeCe Winans. Nor the anointing and longevity of Shirley Caesar or the powerful volume and anointed subtlety of Maranda Curtis and I definitely have not excelled to musical and pharyngeal acrobatics of Kim Burrell, but when I am suitably inspired to sing I can hold a note and most times find a harmony!

I can remember that as a little girl I loved singing and making up my own songs. As I grew older, I didn't sing as much but over the last few years my passion for singing has been rekindled. I can't say that my inspirations could win me a Stellar Award or one of my creations find itself in the Top 20 of any Gospel Music Chart but that's ok – I'm not aiming for human recognition and accolades. These days all I am interested in is matching my singing with the sound of my affliction and hoping and praying that it touches God's heart.

So I sing in my kitchen. I sing in my bathroom. I sing in my car. I sing in my office. I sing in my church services. I sing while walking or sitting and on occasion I have even awoken out my sleep singing. I sing when I am happy. I sing when I am sad. I sing in my difficult times. I sing in my struggles and I also sing in my times of suffering and affliction. The words of another one of my favourite hymns comes to mind:

When peace, like a river, attendeth my way,[82]
When sorrows like sea billows roll;
Whatever my lot, Thou hast taught me to say,
It is well, it is well with my soul.

Refrain:
It is well with my soul,
It is well, it is well with my soul.

Though Satan should buffet,
though trials should come,
Let this blest assurance control,
That Christ hath regarded my helpless estate,
And hath shed His own blood for my soul.

My sin—oh, the bliss of this glorious thought!—
My sin, not in part but the whole,
Is nailed to the cross, and I bear it no more,
Praise the Lord, praise the Lord, O my soul!

For me, be it Christ, be it Christ hence to live:
If Jordan above me shall roll,
No pang shall be mine, for in death as in life
Thou wilt whisper Thy peace to my soul.

But, Lord, 'tis for Thee, for Thy coming we wait,
The sky, not the grave, is our goal;

Oh, trump of the angel! Oh, voice of the Lord!
Blessed hope, blessed rest of my soul!

And Lord, haste the day
when the faith shall be sight,
The clouds be rolled back as a scroll;
The trump shall resound,
and the Lord shall descend,
Even so, it is well with my soul.

I have come to the conclusion that affliction will always be a part of the believer's life. This is born out in the words of Paul to Corinthians speaking about being constantly in danger of death (2 Corinthians 4:11). So, we will always have to deal with some aspect of suffering as we carry out God's Kingdom work in the Earth but what I have decided is that no matter what I may or may not be going through at any given season in my life I'm going to sing anyway!

This has been quite a journey. I wasn't really sure where I would find myself as I looked into the subject of affliction and its connection to sound. I definitely wasn't prepared for the amount of information I would dig up or the wide range of emotions I would feel while writing.

I'm glad I listened to my husband and took the next step to move forward from the messages I preached to write the book. I have definitely been stirred and undoubtedly deeply inspired and encouraged. I remember when I preached, it resonated in deep places, not just in me but in those who were present. We weren't the same when we left church that Sunday. We left filled with hope and strength knowing that Our God hears us in so many different ways. So I pray that after reading this book your life will be remarkably changed when you consider the fact that **Your Affliction Has A Sound...**

I am definitely in a different place to where I was when I started writing, "My Affliction Has A Sound" and with that in mind I have decided that no matter what, I will refuse to keep silent and I'm going to sing anyway!... and I hope you will too!

Bible Inspired Prayers

The following are some prayers that the people of God who were experiencing affliction in the Bible prayed. They speak from a deep place and an honest place. If ever there comes a time when you feel like you are going through a season of affliction, perhaps reading these prayers will help to remind you no matter how bad the suffering becomes that Jehovah God hears and sees and will in due time answer.

Psalm 102 (New King James Version)

[1] Hear my prayer, O Lord,
And let my cry come to You.
[2] Do not hide Your face from me in the day of my trouble;
Incline Your ear to me;
In the day that I call, answer me speedily.
[3] For my days are consumed like smoke,
And my bones are burned like a hearth.
[4] My heart is stricken and withered like grass,
So that I forget to eat my bread.
[5] Because of the sound of my groaning
My bones cling to my skin.
[6] I am like a pelican of the wilderness;
I am like an owl of the desert.

7 I lie awake,
And am like a sparrow alone on the housetop.
8 My enemies reproach me all day long;
Those who deride me swear an oath against me.
9 For I have eaten ashes like bread,
And mingled my drink with weeping,
10 Because of Your indignation and Your wrath;
For You have lifted me up and cast me away.
11 My days *are* like a shadow that lengthens,
And I wither away like grass.
12 But You, O Lord, shall endure forever,
And the remembrance of Your name to all generations.
13 You will arise *and* have mercy on Zion;
For the time to favor her,
Yes, the set time, has come.
14 For Your servants take pleasure in her stones,
And show favor to her dust.
15 So the nations shall fear the name of the Lord,
And all the kings of the earth Your glory.
16 For the Lord shall build up Zion;
He shall appear in His glory.
17 He shall regard the prayer of the destitute,
And shall not despise their prayer.
18 This will be written for the generation to come,
That a people yet to be created may praise the Lord.
19 For He looked down from the height of His sanctuary;
From heaven the Lord viewed the earth,
20 To hear the groaning of the prisoner,
To release those appointed to death,
21 To declare the name of the Lord in Zion,
And His praise in Jerusalem,

22 When the peoples are gathered together,
And the kingdoms, to serve the Lord.
23 He weakened my strength in the way;
He shortened my days.
24 I said, "O my God,
Do not take me away in the midst of my days;
Your years *are* throughout all generations.
25 Of old You laid the foundation of the earth,
And the heavens *are* the work of Your hands.
26 They will perish, but You will endure;
Yes, they will all grow old like a garment;
Like a cloak You will change them,
And they will be changed.
27 But You *are* the same,
And Your years will have no end.
28 The children of Your servants will continue,
And their descendants will be established before You."

Psalm 141 (New King James Version)

1 Lord, I cry out to You;
Make haste to me!
Give ear to my voice when I cry out to You.
2 Let my prayer be set before You *as* incense,
The lifting up of my hands *as* the evening sacrifice.
3 Set a guard, O Lord, over my mouth;
Keep watch over the door of my lips.
4 Do not incline my heart to any evil thing,
To practice wicked works
With men who work iniquity;
And do not let me eat of their delicacies.
5 Let the righteous strike me;

It shall be a kindness.
And let him rebuke me;
It shall be as excellent oil;
Let my head not refuse it.
For still my prayer *is* against the deeds of the wicked.
6 Their judges are overthrown by the sides of the cliff,
And they hear my words, for they are sweet.
7 Our bones are scattered at the mouth of the grave,
As when one plows and breaks up the earth.
8 But my eyes *are* upon You, O God the Lord;
In You I take refuge;
Do not leave my soul destitute.
9 Keep me from the snares they have laid for me,
And from the traps of the workers of iniquity.
10 Let the wicked fall into their own nets,
While I escape safely.

Psalm 142 (New King James Version)
1 I cry out to the Lord with my voice;
With my voice to the Lord I make my supplication.
2 I pour out my complaint before Him;
I declare before Him my trouble.
3 When my spirit was overwhelmed within me,
Then You knew my path.
In the way in which I walk
They have secretly set a snare for me.
4 Look on *my* right hand and see,
For *there is* no one who acknowledges me;
Refuge has failed me;
No one cares for my soul.

5 I cried out to You, O Lord:
I said, "You *are* my refuge,
My portion in the land of the living.
6 Attend to my cry,
For I am brought very low;
Deliver me from my persecutors,
For they are stronger than I.
7 Bring my soul out of prison,
That I may praise Your name;
The righteous shall surround me,
For You shall deal bountifully with me."

Psalm 143 (New King James Version)

1 Hear my prayer, O Lord,
Give ear to my supplications!
In Your faithfulness answer me,
And in Your righteousness.
2 Do not enter into judgment with Your servant,
For in Your sight no one living is righteous.
3 For the enemy has persecuted my soul;
He has crushed my life to the ground;
He has made me dwell in darkness,
Like those who have long been dead.
4 Therefore my spirit is overwhelmed within me;
My heart within me is distressed.
5 I remember the days of old;
I meditate on all Your works;
I muse on the work of Your hands.
6 I spread out my hands to You;
My soul *longs* for You like a thirsty land. *Selah*
7 Answer me speedily, O Lord;

My spirit fails!
Do not hide Your face from me,
Lest I be like those who go down into the pit.
8 Cause me to hear Your lovingkindness in the morning,
For in You do I trust;
Cause me to know the way in which I should walk,
For I lift up my soul to You.
9 Deliver me, O Lord, from my enemies;
In You I take shelter.
10 Teach me to do Your will,
For You *are* my God;
Your Spirit *is* good.
Lead me in the land of uprightness.
11 Revive me, O Lord, for Your name's sake!
For Your righteousness' sake bring my soul out of trouble.
12 In Your mercy cut off my enemies,
And destroy all those who afflict my soul;
For I *am* Your servant.

Psalm 61 (New King James Version)

1 Hear my cry, O God;
Attend to my prayer.
2 From the end of the earth I will cry to You,
When my heart is overwhelmed;
Lead me to the rock that is higher than I.
3 For You have been a shelter for me,
A strong tower from the enemy.
4 I will abide in Your tabernacle forever;
I will trust in the shelter of Your wings. *Selah*
5 For You, O God, have heard my vows;

You have given *me* the heritage of those who fear Your name.
6 You will prolong the king's life,
His years as many generations.
7 He shall abide before God forever.
Oh, prepare mercy and truth, *which* may preserve him!
8 So I will sing praise to Your name forever,
That I may daily perform my vows.

Psalm 86 (New King James Version)

1 Bow down Your ear, O Lord, hear me;
For I *am* poor and needy.
2 Preserve my life, for I *am* holy;
You are my God;
Save Your servant who trusts in You!
3 Be merciful to me, O Lord,
For I cry to You all day long.
4 Rejoice the soul of Your servant,
For to You, O Lord, I lift up my soul.
5 For You, Lord, *are* good, and ready to forgive,
And abundant in mercy to all those who call upon You.
6 Give ear, O Lord, to my prayer;
And attend to the voice of my supplications.
7 In the day of my trouble I will call upon You,
For You will answer me.
8 Among the gods *there is* none like You, O Lord;
Nor *are there any works* like Your works.
9 All nations whom You have made
Shall come and worship before You, O Lord,
And shall glorify Your name.

¹⁰ For You *are* great, and do wondrous things;
You alone *are* God.
¹¹ Teach me Your way, O Lord;
I will walk in Your truth;
Unite my heart to fear Your name.
¹² I will praise You, O Lord my God, with all my heart,
And I will glorify Your name forevermore.
¹³ For great *is* Your mercy toward me,
And You have delivered my soul from the depths of Sheol.
¹⁴ O God, the proud have risen against me,
And a mob of violent *men* have sought my life,
And have not set You before them.
¹⁵ But You, O Lord, *are* a God full of compassion, and gracious,
Longsuffering and abundant in mercy and truth.
¹⁶ Oh, turn to me, and have mercy on me!
Give Your strength to Your servant,
And save the son of Your maidservant.
¹⁷ Show me a sign for good,
That those who hate me may see *it* and be ashamed,
Because You, Lord, have helped me and comforted me.

Psalm 88 (New King James Version)

¹ O Lord, God of my salvation,
I have cried out day and night before You.
² Let my prayer come before You;
Incline Your ear to my cry.
³ For my soul is full of troubles,
And my life draws near to the grave.
⁴ I am counted with those who go down to the pit;
I am like a man *who has* no strength,

5 Adrift among the dead,
Like the slain who lie in the grave,
Whom You remember no more,
And who are cut off from Your hand.
6 You have laid me in the lowest pit,
In darkness, in the depths.
7 Your wrath lies heavy upon me,
And You have afflicted *me* with all Your waves. *Selah*
8 You have put away my acquaintances far from me;
You have made me an abomination to them;
I am shut up, and I cannot get out;
9 My eye wastes away because of affliction.
Lord, I have called daily upon You;
I have stretched out my hands to You.
10 Will You work wonders for the dead?
Shall the dead arise *and* praise You? *Selah*
11 Shall Your lovingkindness be declared in the grave?
Or Your faithfulness in the place of destruction?
12 Shall Your wonders be known in the dark?
And Your righteousness in the land of forgetfulness?
13 But to You I have cried out, O Lord,
And in the morning my prayer comes before You.
14 Lord, why do You cast off my soul?
Why do You hide Your face from me?
15 I *have been* afflicted and ready to die from *my* youth;
I suffer Your terrors;
I am distraught.
16 Your fierce wrath has gone over me;
Your terrors have cut me off.
17 They came around me all day long like water;
They engulfed me altogether.

18 Loved one and friend You have put far from me,
And my acquaintances into darkness.

Psalm 130 (New King James Version)

1 Out of the depths I have cried to You, O Lord;
2 Lord, hear my voice!
Let Your ears be attentive
To the voice of my supplications.
3 If You, Lord, should mark iniquities,
O Lord, who could stand?
4 But *there is* forgiveness with You,
That You may be feared.
5 I wait for the Lord, my soul waits,
And in His word I do hope.
6 My soul *waits* for the Lord
More than those who watch for the morning—
Yes, more than those who watch for the morning.
7 O Israel, hope in the Lord;
For with the Lord *there is* mercy,
And with Him *is* abundant redemption.
8 And He shall redeem Israel
From all his iniquities.

Psalm 69 (New King James Version)

1 Save me, O God!
For the waters have come up to *my* neck.
2 I sink in deep mire,
Where *there is* no standing;
I have come into deep waters,
Where the floods overflow me.
3 I am weary with my crying;

My throat is dry;
My eyes fail while I wait for my God.
4 Those who hate me without a cause
Are more than the hairs of my head;
They are mighty who would destroy me,
Being my enemies wrongfully;
Though I have stolen nothing,
I *still* must restore *it.*
5 O God, You know my foolishness;
And my sins are not hidden from You.
6 Let not those who wait for You, O Lord God of hosts, be
ashamed because of me;
Let not those who seek You be confounded because of
me, O God of Israel.
7 Because for Your sake I have borne reproach;
Shame has covered my face.
8 I have become a stranger to my brothers,
And an alien to my mother's children;
9 Because zeal for Your house has eaten me up,
And the reproaches of those who reproach You have fallen
on me.
10 When I wept *and chastened* my soul with fasting,
That became my reproach.
11 I also made sackcloth my garment;
I became a byword to them.
12 Those who sit in the gate speak against me,
And I *am* the song of the drunkards.
13 But as for me, my prayer *is* to You,
O Lord, *in* the acceptable time;
O God, in the multitude of Your mercy,
Hear me in the truth of Your salvation.

14 Deliver me out of the mire,
And let me not sink;
Let me be delivered from those who hate me,
And out of the deep waters.
15 Let not the floodwater overflow me,
Nor let the deep swallow me up;
And let not the pit shut its mouth on me.
16 Hear me, O Lord, for Your lovingkindness *is* good;
Turn to me according to the multitude of Your tender
mercies.
17 And do not hide Your face from Your servant,
For I am in trouble;
Hear me speedily.
18 Draw near to my soul, *and* redeem it;
Deliver me because of my enemies.
19 You know my reproach, my shame, and my dishonor;
My adversaries *are* all before You.
20 Reproach has broken my heart,
And I am full of heaviness;
I looked *for someone* to take pity, but *there was* none;
And for comforters, but I found none.
21 They also gave me gall for my food,
And for my thirst they gave me vinegar to drink.
22 Let their table become a snare before them,
And their well-being a trap.
23 Let their eyes be darkened, so that they do not see;
And make their loins shake continually.
24 Pour out Your indignation upon them,
And let Your wrathful anger take hold of them.
25 Let their dwelling place be desolate;
Let no one live in their tents.

26 For they persecute the *ones* You have struck,
And talk of the grief of those You have wounded.

27 Add iniquity to their iniquity,
And let them not come into Your righteousness.
28 Let them be blotted out of the book of the living,
And not be written with the righteous.
29 But I *am* poor and sorrowful;
Let Your salvation, O God, set me up on high.
30 I will praise the name of God with a song,
And will magnify Him with thanksgiving.
31 *This* also shall please the Lord better than an ox *or* bull,
Which has horns and hooves.
32 The humble shall see *this and* be glad;
And you who seek God, your hearts shall live.
33 For the Lord hears the poor,
And does not despise His prisoners.
34 Let heaven and earth praise Him,
The seas and everything that moves in them.
35 For God will save Zion
And build the cities of Judah,
That they may dwell there and possess it.
36 Also, the descendants of His servants shall inherit it,
And those who love His name shall dwell in it.

Psalm 40 (New King James Version)

1 I waited patiently for the Lord;
And He inclined to me,
And heard my cry.
2 He also brought me up out of a horrible pit,
Out of the miry clay,

And set my feet upon a rock,
And established my steps.
3 He has put a new song in my mouth—
Praise to our God;
Many will see *it* and fear,
And will trust in the Lord.
4 Blessed *is* that man who makes the Lord his trust,
And does not respect the proud, nor such as turn aside to
lies.
5 Many, O Lord my God, *are* Your wonderful works
Which You have done;
And Your thoughts toward us
Cannot be recounted to You in order;
If I would declare and speak *of them,*
They are more than can be numbered.
6 Sacrifice and offering You did not desire;
My ears You have opened.
Burnt offering and sin offering You did not require.
7 Then I said, "Behold, I come;
In the scroll of the book *it is* written of me.
8 I delight to do Your will, O my God,
And Your law *is* within my heart."
9 I have proclaimed the good news of righteousness
In the great assembly;
Indeed, I do not restrain my lips,
O Lord, You Yourself know.
10 I have not hidden Your righteousness within my heart;
I have declared Your faithfulness and Your salvation;
I have not concealed Your lovingkindness and Your truth
From the great assembly.

11 Do not withhold Your tender mercies from me, O Lord;
Let Your lovingkindness and Your truth continually
preserve me.
12 For innumerable evils have surrounded me;
My iniquities have overtaken me, so that I am not able to
look up;
They are more than the hairs of my head;
Therefore my heart fails me.
13 Be pleased, O Lord, to deliver me;
O Lord, make haste to help me!
14 Let them be ashamed and brought to mutual confusion
Who seek to destroy my life;
Let them be driven backward and brought to dishonor
Who wish me evil.
15 Let them be confounded because of their shame,
Who say to me, "Aha, aha!"
16 Let all those who seek You rejoice and be glad in You;
Let such as love Your salvation say continually,
"The Lord be magnified!"
17 But I *am* poor and needy;
Yet the Lord thinks upon me.
You *are* my help and my deliverer;
Do not delay, O my God.

Psalm 28 (New King James Version)
1 To You I will cry, O Lord my Rock:
Do not be silent to me,
Lest, if You *are* silent to me,
I become like those who go down to the pit.
2 Hear the voice of my supplications
When I cry to You,

When I lift up my hands toward Your holy sanctuary.
3 Do not take me away with the wickedAnd with the workers of iniquity,
Who speak peace to their neighbors,
But evil *is* in their hearts.
4 Give them according to their deeds,
And according to the wickedness of their endeavors;
Give them according to the work of their hands;
Render to them what they deserve.
5 Because they do not regard the works of the Lord,
Nor the operation of His hands,
He shall destroy them
And not build them up.
6 Blessed *be* the Lord,
Because He has heard the voice of my supplications!
7 The Lord *is* my strength and my shield;
My heart trusted in Him, and I am helped;
Therefore my heart greatly rejoices,
And with my song I will praise Him.
8 The Lord *is* their strength,
And He *is* the saving refuge of His anointed.
9 Save Your people,
And bless Your inheritance;
Shepherd them also,
And bear them up forever.

Your Personal Prayers & Thoughts

Use the following pages to write your own thoughts and prayers and personal testimonies of God's providence to you during and after your seasons of affliction.

_____

_____

_____

_____

_____

_____

_____

_____

_____

_____

_____

_____

Your Personal Prayers & Thoughts

Use the following pages to write your own thoughts and prayers and personal testimonies of God's providence to you during and after your seasons of affliction.

_____

_____

_____

_____

_____

_____

_____

_____

_____

_____

_____

_____

_____

Your Personal Prayers & Thoughts

Use the following pages to write your own thoughts and prayers and personal testimonies of God's providence to you during and after your seasons of affliction.

_____

_____

_____

_____

_____

_____

_____

_____

_____

_____

_____

_____

Your Personal Prayers & Thoughts

Use the following pages to write your own thoughts and prayers and personal testimonies of God's providence to you during and after your seasons of affliction.

_____

_____

_____

_____

_____

_____

_____

_____

_____

_____

_____

_____

_____

Your Personal Prayers & Thoughts

Use the following pages to write your own thoughts and prayers and personal testimonies of God's providence to you during and after your seasons of affliction.

_____

_____

_____

_____

_____

_____

_____

_____

_____

_____

_____

_____

_____

Your Personal Prayers & Thoughts

Use the following pages to write your own thoughts and prayers and personal testimonies of God's providence to you during and after your seasons of affliction.

_____

_____

_____

_____

_____

_____

_____

_____

_____

_____

_____

_____

Your Personal Prayers & Thoughts

Use the following pages to write your own thoughts and prayers and personal testimonies of God's providence to you during and after your seasons of affliction.

_____

_____

_____

_____

_____

_____

_____

_____

_____

_____

_____

_____

Your Personal Prayers & Thoughts

Use the following pages to write your own thoughts and prayers and personal testimonies of God's providence to you during and after your seasons of affliction.

_____

_____

_____

_____

_____

_____

_____

_____

_____

_____

_____

_____

_____

_____

Your Personal Prayers & Thoughts

Use the following pages to write your own thoughts and prayers and personal testimonies of God's providence to you during and after your seasons of affliction.

_____

_____

_____

_____

_____

_____

_____

_____

_____

_____

_____

_____

_____

Your Personal Prayers & Thoughts

Use the following pages to write your own thoughts and prayers and personal testimonies of God's providence to you during and after your seasons of affliction.

_____

_____

_____

_____

_____

_____

_____

_____

_____

_____

_____

_____

_____

_____

Your Personal Prayers & Thoughts

Use the following pages to write your own thoughts and prayers and personal testimonies of God's providence to you during and after your seasons of affliction.

_____

_____

_____

_____

_____

_____

_____

_____

_____

_____

_____

_____

_____

Your Personal Prayers & Thoughts

Use the following pages to write your own thoughts and prayers and personal testimonies of God's providence to you during and after your seasons of affliction.

_____

_____

_____

_____

_____

_____

_____

_____

_____

_____

_____

_____

_____

_____

Reference Sources

An Affliction Story
1. Jewish Bible Quarterly
   http://jbqnew.jewishbible.org/assets/Uploads/414/JBQ_4
   14_1_angelhagar.pdf
2. Jewish Bible Quarterly
   http://jbqnew.jewishbible.org/assets/Uploads/414/JBQ_4
   14_1_angelhagar.pdf

What is Affliction?
3. Strong's Concordance Reference Numbers:
   OT: 6040 `oniy' - depression, i.e. misery
   OT: 6031 'aniy' - depressed, in mind or circumstances
   OT: 6030 'anah' - the idea of looking down or browbeating

Affliction Connected to Music
4. Strong's Concordance Reference Number: OT:6030
   `anah (aw-naw') - to begin to speak; specifically to sing,
   shout, testify, announce ...cry, hear, Leannoth, lift up, say,
   scholar, (give a) shout, sing (together by course)
5. Strabo: Greek geographer and historian
   https://en.wikipedia.org/wiki/Strabo

What is Sound?
6. Definition of sound
   https://en.oxforddictionaries.com/definition/sound
7. Article: Sound
   https://en.wikipedia.org/wiki/Sound_(disambiguation)
8. Why sound is important
   https://www.reference.com/science/sound
9. Article: Sound
   https://en.wikipedia.org/wiki/Sound
10. Article: Sound
    https://en.wikipedia.org/wiki/Sound

More to Sound than Meets the Ear

11. Review of the atom
https://www.nde-d.org/EducationResources/HighSchool/Magnetism/reviewatom.htm

12. The Law of Three
https://www.facebook.com/fortunatepeoplesmile/posts/1060122787335653

13. The number 3 in scripture
http://www.agapebiblestudy.com/documents/The%20Significance%20of%20Numbers%20in%20Scripture.htm

14. Aura
https://en.oxforddictionaries.com/definition/aura

15. Body in motion
https://en.wikipedia.org/wiki/Motion_(physics)

16. Newton's Laws of Motion
https://en.wikipedia.org/wiki/Newton's_laws_of_motion

17. Laws of Thermodynamics
https://en.wikipedia.org/wiki/Laws_of_thermodynamics

The Science of Cymatics

18. The Science of Cymatics
https://en.wikipedia.org/wiki/Cymatics

19. Hans Jenny
https://en.wikipedia.org/wiki/Hans_Jenny_(cymatics)

20. Ernst Chladni
https://en.wikipedia.org/wiki/Ernst_Chladni

21. Chladni figures
https://en.wikipedia.org/wiki/Ernst_Chladni#Chladni_figures

22. Galileo
https://en.wikipedia.org/wiki/Galileo_Galilei

23. Robert Hooke
https://en.wikipedia.org/wiki/Robert_Hooke

24. Mandala
http://www.mandalaproject.org/What/Index.html

25. Developments in the science of cymatics
   https://ask.audio/articles/how-sound-affects-you-cymatics-an-emerging-science
26. English Acoustics Engineer John Stuart Reid and Design
   Engineer Erik Larson
   https://www.cymascope.com/cyma_research/Veritas_cymatics.pdf
27. CymaPiano (image)
   http://www.cymascope.com/cyma_research/musicology.html
28. CymaScope App
   https://cymascope.com/cyma_research/cyma_app.html

Sound Therapy — Science or Myth?

29. Article: Sound Therapy
   https://www.theguardian.com/lifeandstyle/2008/jul/06/healthandwellbeing5
30. Responses to music
   http://www.cerebromente.org.br/n15/mente/musica.html
31. The British Academy of Sound Therapy
   http://www.britishacademyofsoundtherapy.com/
32. Bone fracture healing
   https://www.ncbi.nlm.nih.gov/pmc/articles/PMC2748418

Sympathetic Resonance

33. Sympathetic resonance
   http://www.physlink.com/education/askexperts/ae479.cfm
34. Opera singer breaks glass
   http://www.acoustics.salford.ac.uk/acoustics_info/glass/
35. Holy Spirit groans
   Strong's Concordance Reference Number: NT:4727
   stenazo (sten-ad'-zo)

I Hear a Sound

36 Help my unbelief - Mark 9:17-24
37. No rain on the earth for 3 years - 1 kings 17:1;
   1 Kings 18:1
38. Idol worship - 1 Kings 16:33

39. Elijah cared for by ravens and a widow - 1 kings 17
40. Elijah challenges prophets of Baal - 1 Kings 18

"Leannoth" — Let's Sing Together
41. Telegraph Newspaper Article: Singing Together
    https://www.telegraph.co.uk/news/health/10168914/All-together-now-singing-is-good-for-your-body-and-soul.html
42. The father heals - Exodus 15:26
    Strong's Concordance Reference Number: OT: 7495 -
    rapha' or raphah
43. Paul and Silas - Acts 16
44. Tibetan monks chant
    https://en.wikipedia.org/wiki/Overtone_singing
45. Mongolian Chanting/Overtone singing
    https://en.wikipedia.org/wiki/Tuvan_throat_singing
46. Music and worship in the temple
    http://www.biblelessons.com/origins.html

47. Heaven, the pattern for worship - Hebrews 8:5;
    Hebrews 9:23
48. Worship God in spirit and truth - John 4:23-24

Music Therapy — An Alternative Miracle?
49. Music Therapy
    http://www.cancerresearchuk.org/about-cancer/cancers-in-general/treatment/complementary-alternative/therapies/music-therapy
50. Music Therapy - 7 ways
    https://mic.com/articles/133981/7-ways-music-affects-the-body-here-s-how-science-says-sound-moves-us#.pv5bmn9bz
51. Gottfried Schlaug
    https://newsinhealth.nih.gov/2010/january/feature1.htm
52. Frontiers in Psychology in 2013
    https://www.ncbi.nlm.nih.gov/pmc/articles/PMC4513245
53. Dawn Kent
    http://digitalcommons.liberty.edu/cgi/viewcontent.cgi?article=1162&context=honors

54. Michelle Lefevre
http://www.academia.edu/26636131/Playing_with_sound_The_therapeutic_use_of_music_in_direct_work_with_children
55. The Mozart Effect
https://www.epilepsy.org.uk/info/treatment/effects-of-other-things-on-treatment/mozart-effect
56. Curtis Levang
http://www.everydayhealth.com/low-testosterone/music-for-low-t-get-in-tune-with-your-sex-drive.aspx
57. Spotify running
https://www.spotify.com/uk/running/
58. Dr Jerry Saliman
http://www.jweekly.com/2016/01/29/singing-is-good-for-your-health-good-for-your-soul/
59. Music Therapy - 10 ways
http://www.viralnovelty.net/10-powerful-effects-music-body-mind-soul/
60. Song of loves: Heading of Psalm 45:1
61. Song of fools: Ecclesiastes 7:5
62. Song of Songs: Song of Solomon 1:1
63. Song of the Lamb: Revelation 15:3
64. Song of the Lord: 2 Chronicles 29:27
65. Song of degrees: Headings of Psalm 120 - Psalm 134
66. Song of Moses: Revelation 15:3
67. Song of Asaph: Psalm 75:1; Psalm 76:1
68. Sweet Hour of Prayer - Author: W. W. Walford (1845)
69. My Jesus, I love Thee: Author: William R. Featherstone (1864)
70. There is a land of pure delight - Author: Isaac Watts (1709)
71. I need Thee every hour Author: Annie S. Hawks (1872) Author (refrain): Robert Lowry (1872)
72. Guide me, O Thou great Jehovah Author: William Williams (1745); Translator: Peter Williams (1771)
73. Father, I stretch my hands to thee - Author: Charles Wesley
74. Miguel de Cervantes 1547–1616)
https://en.wikipedia.org/wiki/Miguel_de_Cervantes

Affliction is Good!
75. Dross
    https://www.merriam-webster.com/dictionary/dross

Sing Anyway!
76 Affliction - Mark 13:19
    Strong's Concordance Reference Numbers:
    NT:2347 thlipsis (thlip'-sis)
77. Larynx
    http://www.dummies.com/education/science/anatomy/
    the-pharynx-larynx-and-trachea/

78. The Science of Singing
    https://www.theguardian.com/lifeandstyle/2014/jun/19/s
    cience-singing-how-our-brains-bodies-produce-sound
79. Left and right hemisphere of the brain
    www.ronitbaras.com/emotional-intelligence/personal-
    development/happiness-is-in-the-right-brain/
80. Zoltán Kodály (1882-1967)-Hungarian composer,
    ethnomusicologist, pedagogue, linguist, and philosopher.
81. James 5:13 - 'Let him pray'
    Strong's Concordance Reference Numbers: NT:4336
    proseuchomai (pros-yoo'-khom-ahee)
82. It Is Well with My Soul - Horatio G. Spafford (1873)

Ministry Contact Information

Website

www.pastorpennyfrancis.com

Phone

Ruach City Church

+44 (020) 8678 6888

Email

global@ruachcitychurch.org

PENNY FRANCIS

FOREWORD BY BISHOP JOHN FRANCIS

My affliction has a SOUND

Discover the powerful connection between sound and our suffering

Lightning Source UK Ltd.
Milton Keynes UK
UKHW022021041019
351019UK00002B/9/P